T·H·E
NEW MARINE
AQUARIUM

STEP-BY-STEP SETUP & STOCKING GUIDE

Front Cover
Banggai Cardinalfish (*Pterapogon kauderni*)
Photograph by Scott W. Michael

Back Cover
Top: Aquarium setup illustration by Edward Kadunc
Middle: Custom aquarium by Jeffrey Turner, Exotic Aquaria / ORA. Photograph by Steve Lucas
Bottom (species photographs):
Top left: Ocellaris Clownfish (*Amphiprion ocellaris*); Top right: Royal Gramma (*Gramma loreto*);
Bottom left: Redspotted Blenny (*Istiblennius chrysospilos*); Bottom right: South Seas Devil Damselfish (*Chrysiptera taupou*).
Photographs by Scott W. Michael

Produced and distributed by
T.F.H. Publications, Inc.
One TFH Plaza
Third and Union Avenues
Neptune City, NJ 07753
www.tfh.com

T·H·E
NEW MARINE
AQUARIUM

STEP-BY-STEP SETUP & STOCKING GUIDE

MICHAEL S. PALETTA

ILLUSTRATIONS BY EDWARD KADUNC

PRINCIPAL PHOTOGRAPHERS:
SCOTT W. MICHAEL & JOHN GOODMAN

MICROCOSM

tfh

PROFESSIONAL
SERIES™

T.F.H. Publications
One TFH Plaza
Third and Union Avenues
Neptune City, NJ 07753
www.tfh.com

This book has been published with the intent to provide accurate and authoritative
information in regard to the subject matter within. While every precaution has been
taken in preparation of this book, the publisher and author assume no responsibility for errors
or omissions. Neither is any liability assumed for damages resulting from
the use of the information herein.

ISBN 1-890087-52-1 (pbk.)

Printed and bound in the United States of America

Library of Congress Cataloging-in-Publication Data
Paletta, Michael S.
The new marine aquarium: step-by-step setup & stocking guide/
by Michael S. Paletta.
   p.   cm.
Includes bibliographical references and index.
ISBN 1-890087-52-1 (pbk.)
1. Marine aquariums. I. Title.
SF457.1.P35 1998   98-34407
639.34'2—dc21   CIP

Color separations by Digital Media Inc. U.S.A., Grants Pass, Oregon
Designed by Eugenie Seidenberg Delaney

Co-published by
Microcosm Ltd.
P.O. Box 550
Charlotte, VT 05445
www.microcosm-books.com

To my family—especially my grandmother and parents,
who nurtured my love of aquariums over the years—
and to my wife and children who abide my aquatic passions.

■ ■ ■

ACKNOWLEDGMENTS

HELP, SUPPORT, AND INVALUABLE information have been provided to me by many individuals over the years. Their advice and generous sharing of knowledge have guided me both with my writing and with the evolution of my own aquariums.

My sincere thanks go to: Parker Adams, Sam Angil, Vince Apauron, Ed Bauman, Jimmy Boswell, John Burleson, Tony Calfo, Dr. Bruce Carlson, Greg Cook, Chris Cortese, Charles Delbeek, Peter J. Dziadyk, Dale Fox, Dirk Griffith, LeRoy and Sally Jo Headlee, Dave Herr, Dr. Rob Hildreth, Roy Hoover, Ron Hunsiker, Bob James, Dave Jancetic, Kelly Jedlicki, Sanjay Joshi, Stuart Keefer, Doug Kevis, Millie Klevens, Jack Lentz, Dr. Peter Linden, Kurt Loos, Jeff Macaré, Tom Majocha, Bob Mankin, Joy and Gary Meadows, Greg Meeker, Martin A. Moe, Jr., Edmund Mowka, Gary Myers, Valerie Nahay, Alf Jacob Nilsen, Teresa Elaine Pallone, Dick Perrin, Dana Riddle, Greg Sachs, Greg Scheimer, Mark Scott, Terry Seigel, Wayne Shang, Greg Smith, Julian Sprung, Bob Stark, Howard Swimmer, Leng Sy, Perry Tishgart, Frank Tosto, Steve Tyree, Tony Vargas, Penny Williams, Dave Wodecki, Kathleen Wood, and Joe Yaiullo.

I am especially grateful to Jeff Voet (of Tropical Fish World in Raleigh, North Carolina), Tom Frakes (of Aquarium Systems), Bob Fenner, and Richard Harker, not only for suggesting improvements to my manuscript, but also for their expertise in answering innumerable questions during its preparation.

Many people played a role in assembling this book, and I wish to thank illustrator Edward Kadunc, photographer John Goodman, designer Eugenie Seidenberg Delaney, and everyone at Microcosm. This book would not have been the same without Scott Michael's involvement and his wonderful species photographs. I would also like to acknowledge the help of Jeffrey Turner, of Oceans Reefs & Aquariums, Palm Beach, Florida, and Steve Lucas for providing photographs of live-rock-based marine systems. Thanks as well to Teresa and Roy Herndon of Sea Critters in Dover, Florida, and Dennis Reynolds of Aqua Marines in Hermosa Beach, California, for providing numerous samples of live rock and sand to be photographed.

Finally, I am very grateful to Jim Prappas and Ken Billin of the Pittsburgh Zoo Aquarium, Ed and Brian Taimuty of Wet Pets Pet Shop, and Dr. Michael Fontana and Dr. Ron Cypher for taking time from their busy schedules and allowing us to photograph their beautiful tanks in their homes and businesses.

CONTENTS

PREFACE

What is "The New Marine Aquarium"?

As BEDAZZLING AS ANY ENVIRONMENT ON Earth, the coral reef has caught the eye—and the imagination—of a new wave of aquarium keepers.

Using natural biological processes learned from the reef itself and some simple but ingenious new equipment, saltwater aquarists can now capture a slice of underwater nature in a beautiful home aquarium system.

Success, however, means evading some entrenched methods in favor of a new—but well-tested—technique that makes for longer, healthier lives for reef fishes, more authentic aquascaping, and easier long-term maintenance.

In short, the way is now open for many more hobbyists to discover the unique rewards of creating and keeping a saltwater aquarium—and at the same time make a personal link to one of our planet's most astonishing natural realms.

INTRODUCTION

A Better Way to Simpler, Healthier,
More Beautiful Marine Aquariums

LIKE A LIVING KALEIDOSCOPE, A MARINE aquarium brings us face-to-face with some of nature's most beautiful fishes and incredible undersea life forms, offering a window on a world many of us will never visit. With a daily spectacle provided by dazzling coral reef creatures, a sparkling saltwater system can be a dynamic presence in a home, office, or classroom. It can be riveting, educational, and uniquely soothing to observers of all ages—and may even become a lifelong passion for the person who creates it.

Curious humans have kept sea life in small bodies of water for millennia—the ancient Romans had *maritimae* (small saltwater ponds) in which they housed Mediterranean invertebrates and fishes, for both view-

Left: the author's 480-gallon reef tank, with live rock as the filtration mainstay. **Above:** Flame Hawkfish (*Neocirrhites armatus*).

ing and fresh table fare. (There are reports of sizable moray eels being kept, sometimes in pits into which troublesome slaves could be thrown.) Nineteenth-century British gentry kept many forms of temperate tidal life, including cold-water anemones, in a variety of containers, including inverted bell jars.

The real age of marine fishkeeping, however, has very recent origins. The popularization of scuba equipment in the mid-twentieth century suddenly opened the undersea world to study and collection, and interest in marine aquariums has blossomed in the decades since. The formulation of synthetic salt mixes, allowing landlocked hobbyists to create a viable substitute for natural seawater, was a major advance of the 1950s. Growing airline connections to the island nations of the Tropics opened supply lines for marine livestock. European and North American inventors and manufacturers responded to consumer demands for better aquariums, mechanical

Old-style marine aquarium, utilizing dead coral skeletons, which are destined to become overgrown with unsightly algae and whose collection is opposed by many biologists.

They were even buying my home-bred exotic Tanganyikan Cichlid offspring. When I pressed to discover why they were trying to dissuade me, the reply was discouraging. They said that marine tanks were difficult and expensive, that they required a lot of specialized equipment, and that, despite the expense, the fishes often died after a short time.

Undaunted, I decided to try anyway. It has now been almost 20 years since I set up that first tank. Needless to say, I was stubborn enough to prove them at least partly wrong, but along the way I did discover that some of what they said was correct. It was more expensive to set up a marine tank, not to mention how pricey the fish were and how, when anything went wrong, the most expensive specimen always seemed to be the first to go. However, after 5 years and literally thousands of dollars I began achieving a modicum of success. My fishes were usually living for at least 6 months and I was no longer having the whole population die off mysteriously. Granted, the algae on the dead coral skeletons and glass had to be cleaned frequently, and the entire tank needed to be broken down every year or so in order for the sand and undergravel filter to be cleaned. In terms of keeping a saltwater fish tank at that time, what I was doing was messy but pretty much state of the art.

In truth, if it weren't for the incredible beauty and fascinating behaviors of coral reef fishes and invertebrates, I probably would have given up just as so many other saltwater hobbyists did. With what we knew then, keeping a marine aquarium demanded deep pockets, a willingness to learn by experimentation, and a tremendous sense of dedication to keep going.

gear, and foods. Never before has the would-be aquarium keeper had such a breadth of choice among equipment, livestock, and aquascaping materials—ranging from lights and controllers that emulate tropical sunshine and moonlight to never-before-seen reef fishes, live colonies of stony corals, and biologically rich reef rock and coral sand.

IMPOSSIBLE DREAMS?

STILL, IT IS COMMON TO HEAR that saltwater fishes are extremely challenging—if not impossible—to maintain in home aquarium systems. As with many aquarists, I was irreversibly hooked by the brilliant colors and movements of reef fishes, and I first approached the staff of my local aquarium shop in 1980 and told them I wanted to set up a marine fish tank. Rather than warmly welcoming me into the world of marine aquariums, their first words were: "You don't want to do saltwater . . . it's too difficult."

I was astonished—I had shopped there for more than 10 years as a freshwater hobbyist, and they knew that I was successfully keeping and breeding freshwater fishes.

REEF SECRETS

THEN, IN 1986, after seeing photographs of some European tanks, my entire perspective changed. Here were marine aquariums brimming with life—green plants, colorful live rock, and billowing soft corals—and truly starting to mimic the appearance of a coral reef. These were the first popularized "miniature-reef" tanks, where the thrust was in keeping marine invertebrates. The fishes in these tanks were scarce—almost an afterthought. Some reef aquarists even eliminated fishes altogether. These systems utilized stronger lighting and more elaborate filtration methods than anything I had ever seen, with the explanation that corals and marine invertebrates were thought to be much more difficult to maintain than fishes. Like many other aquarists, I was intrigued by the possibilities and began my own research into the new mini-reef techniques.

I've now been working with reef aquariums for more than a decade, and my latest home system is a 480-gallon stony coral tank with more than 100 species of live coral and a collection of fishes that includes pygmy angelfishes; fairy, flasher, and leopard wrasses; moray eels; and a mated pair of clownfish with their host anemone. In the past decade, we have seen many advances that make the keeping of these animals—once thought unkeepable—within our reach.

Filtration systems have evolved in many directions, some becoming highly complex but many others turning toward elegant simplicity. Lighting systems now do a much better job of replicating sunlight, both in terms of spectrum and intensity. In fact, there are now even small computers specifically designed to run these reef tanks (controlling pumps, lights, water chemistry, and providing constant readings on the status of the system) without the need for much intervention by their owners at all.

Most of all, marine reef aquariums are now biologi-

Full of life and vibrant colors, a contemporary marine aquarium displays the results of employing live rock and up-to-date equipment. With enhanced water circulation, protein skimming, and better lighting, many reef organisms can now be kept in home aquariums.

cally richer and their inhabitants are often able to survive for years. Among reef aquarists, it is not unusual to hear of fishes and corals living 5, 10, or even more years in captivity. Amateur aquarists are now propagating many soft and stony corals and a growing number of reef fish species. It is possible to stock a marine aquarium entirely with commercially propagated materials and specimens, including live rock, soft corals, stony corals, gorgonians, gobies, clownfishes, dottybacks, grammas, comets, cardinalfishes, giant clams, and more.

BREAKTHROUGH FOR BEGINNERS

UNFORTUNATELY, the beginning hobbyist has been almost forgotten in this rush to create the ultimate reef aquarium. In terms of innovations and advice for keeping a first marine tank—usually a "fish-only" aquarium—very little has changed. An undergravel filter is still touted as the filtration method of choice for most beginners. This equipment is available everywhere fish tanks are sold, it is cheap to acquire, and nearly a half century of use seems to have made it the unshakable standard. Those who sell them tend to believe in undergravel filters as idiot-proof and akin to training wheels for children learning to ride bikes.

However, what sort of start are we really giving these eager marine newcomers? The unfortunate answer can be found in the pet industry's own statistics: 40 to 60% of all beginning saltwater hobbyists leave the hobby within two years of starting, despite all of the improvements in equipment, the quality of livestock, and our understanding of their needs that have been made over the last decade. The same retail stores that steer their new marine customers to undergravel filters and the traditional bleached coral decorations that go with them will still often warn their clients that saltwater fishkeeping is difficult and expen-

> "NEVER BEFORE HAS THE WOULD-BE AQUARIUM KEEPER HAD SUCH A BREADTH OF CHOICE AMONG EQUIPMENT, LIVESTOCK, AND AQUASCAPING MATERIALS—RANGING FROM LIGHTS AND CONTROLLERS THAT EMULATE TROPICAL SUNSHINE AND MOONLIGHT TO NEVER-BEFORE-SEEN REEF FISHES, LIVE COLONIES OF STONY CORALS, AND BIOLOGICALLY RICH REEF ROCK AND CORAL SAND."
>
> ■ ■ ■

sive. The fishes, we continue to hear, are hard to keep alive for long periods of time. These classic words of caution—the very same problems I had been warned about many years ago—are still being presented to dampen the enthusiasm of eager, would-be marine aquarists.

Curiously, a very interesting development has emerged from the ongoing fascination with reef aquariums. In my own case, I began to notice that the fishes in my reef tanks were living longer and appearing healthier—an unintended by-product of changing my techniques and equipment for the keeping of corals. My tanks are now better maintained and more closely replicate a tiny portion of a reef, and the fishes are doing dramatically better as well.

Having been involved in setting up scores of saltwater systems and visiting aquarists across the country, I believe we now know enough to get new marine hobbyists off to a much better start—without all the complications and expense of setting up a full-blown reef tank. Using a better basic approach to filtration, it should now be possible to let marine fishes live out their full lifespans rather than having to replace them when they perish prematurely. Without these painful and expensive losses, fewer aquarium keepers will become discouraged and depart the hobby for other pursuits.

With this book I hope to demonstrate how to plan, equip, and establish a marine fish tank to those just coming into the saltwater hobby—as well as to anyone who has struggled or failed after using the old standard formula. The method I advocate is not revolutionary—it has been proved reliable in thousands of home aquariums—but it is seldom recommended to novices. The radical part is that it skips immediately past the undergravel filter to the live rock filtration approach that makes reef aquariums work so well.

A full-blown reef aquarium created by Wayne Shang of Fremont, California festooned with live corals and colorful *Tridacna* clams.

A LIVE ROCK METHOD
FOR THE NEW AQUARIST

THE FUNDAMENTALS OF THIS SYSTEM ARE:

1. Live rock as the primary biological filter.

2. Vigorous water circulation to promote gas exchange (including oxygenation) and efficient biological filtration.

3. Nutrient export to remove wastes from the tank (by a combination of protein skimming, optional mechanical filtration, and small, regular water changes).

While an aura of mystery seems to surround it, live rock is nothing more than pieces of old coral rubble collected from shallow tropical seas on or near reefs and shipped damp to preserve the hardy organisms that cover and penetrate it. Good live rock can be festooned with life—sponges, green macroalgae, lovely calcareous algae, crustaceans, mollusks, even small corals—but at the very least, it comes loaded with beneficial microbial cultures that will help maintain healthy aquarium water. The best live rock is irregular in shape, porous, and much more complex than a typical dense river stone. It is, in fact, more like a calcified sponge, full of nooks and crannies and impregnated with beneficial bacterial populations

that can make short work of dissolved aquarium wastes.

A live rock marine setup is as simple to create as the old undergravel filter method and considerably more foolproof. Once established, it is a lower-maintenance system that can operate successfully for years without a need to tear everything down completely for cleaning. A simple arrangement of live rock makes an extremely stable biological filter, better able to facilitate the complete conversion of dissolved wastes and capable of carrying larger fish loads. I believe that fishes in a live rock system consistently live longer, act more natural, and show better colors. Even species previously considered difficult to keep or delicate will often settle into a live rock aquarium and thrive.

FILTRATION PITFALL

IN SHORT, we now have a simple, natural replacement for the undergravel filter. I realize that this will sound like heresy to some retail store personnel and old-time saltwater enthusiasts. Many seem to recommend the undergravel filter out of habit or familiarity—like manual typewriters and wooden downhill skis, the undergravel filter occupies an affectionate spot in some people's hearts. It was a brilliant invention for its time. Realistically, however, time and science have passed by these once-great examples of technology. (Ask a group of experienced marine hobbyists how many are still using undergravel filters. The answer is effectively "none.")

The undergravel filter may always be appropriate for certain freshwater and specialty marine aquariums, but as an essential piece of gear for the average new marine aquarist, it has failed to pass the test of time. As we will discuss in the next chapter, the inescapable flaw of the undergravel filter is that it concentrates solid pollutants and becomes a hard-to-clean sink for all the undissolved wastes in the aquarium, causing a buildup of nitrate to fuel unattractive algae growth and eventually drag water quality down to unacceptably low levels. Undergravel filters are plagued by performance problems—declining circulation causes loss of filtration efficiency and even leads to the development of toxic, anaerobic areas that generate deadly hydrogen sulfide gas.

> "IT IS NOT SIMPLY A MATTER OF SPENDING MORE MONEY TO BE SUCCESSFUL . . . IT IS A FUNCTION OF USING AN APPROACH THAT WORKS—AND AVOIDING ONE THAT DOES NOT."
>
> ■ ■ ■

Do you, as a newcomer to marine aquariums, need to know all of this? Probably not. The important point is to understand that there is a better, simpler way—and that many saltwater fishes are no longer terribly difficult or impossible to keep. The "trick" is nothing more than starting with a system that is self-adjusting and designed for the long haul. With the simplified methods, equipment, and fish species introduced in this book, I firmly believe that the success rate for new marine hobbyists ought to rise to more than 90%, and the needless loss of fishes should decline significantly.

COSTS & BENEFITS

THE COST OF LIVE ROCK will cause the initial investment in a marine setup to increase beyond that of an undergravel system, but this comes with a relatively sure and quick payback. With long-term success of the live rock approach, the cost should eventually be spread out over a longer period of time. One of the highest out-of-pocket expenses of failing aquariums is the need to replace fishes that perish, and a beginner taking this new approach should be spared much of this pain. (It doesn't take the death of too many prized specimens to add up to the additional cost of live rock that might have prevented their demise.) It's not really the expense that pains us most, rather it is the sense that we have failed to provide adequately for our fishes' well-being. One of the worst feelings for an aquarist is having to flush a beautiful fish down the drain—especially if better care might have saved it.

Please understand that it is not simply a matter of spending more money to be successful, as you can follow this method on as large or small a tank as you like. Rather, it is a function of using an approach that works—and avoiding one that does not. In addition to using this new technology you will also have to exercise a bit of patience. Impatience is one of the most difficult attributes to overcome in terms of fishkeeping, as everyone wants to see the tank finished and have the feeling of being successful immediately.

Realistically, it can easily take 6 months to stabilize a tank and probably another 6 months for a new aquarium to be completely established for the long haul. There is a saying that "nothing good ever happens fast in a marine tank." This holds true more often than not. Of course, a new marine aquarium can be interesting and viewable in short order, but it will likely take some months before it starts to become the thing of beauty you may be imagining. (For anyone who insists on overnight results, I would suggest hiring an experienced professional to install and maintain your aquarium. This will not, however, be inexpensive.)

YEARS OF REWARD

FOR THE TRUE HOME AQUARIST creating his or her own system, I think it's very important that you see this project as more than a few weekends of diversion. A tankful of fishes may be less demanding than a dog, cat, or

Marine aquarium aquascape, with a Rainford's Goby (*Amblygobius rainfordi*), which thrives only if able to forage in reeflike conditions.

horse, but the same sense of responsibility for the well-being of a live animal ought to apply. If you aren't willing to make a long-term commitment to the success of your marine aquarium and the consistent care of its living inhabitants, this is not the hobby for you.

On the other hand, if you find the attraction of marine fishes and other organisms irresistible, this could become a lifelong passion as it has for so many others. Watching fishes is a time-tested stress reliever, and many of us find the rituals of feeding and maintenance relaxing and satisfying.

To be a successful marine aquarist demands at least a modest investment of your time, intelligence, money, energy, and creativity. In return, it allows you to exercise any pent-up desires you may have to be a marine zoologist, biochemist, hydraulic engineer, plumber, nutritionist, and/or aquascape designer. Many marine aquarists also find that their aquarium opens a feeling of direct connection to farflung coral reefs and exotic tropical ecosystems, leading many to take up diving, snorkeling, and adventure travel. I can almost guarantee that a marine aquarium will keep you challenged and continually exposed to new ideas and fresh insights for as long as you stay involved. In my own case, after several decades of setting up and observing aquariums, I still consider myself to be on the steep upward slope of my own personal learning curve. I enjoy experimenting and dealing with scientific challenges where there are often more mysteries than answers.

Entering the world of saltwater aquariums can be both exciting and the start of a personal voyage. I hope this book eases the passage and helps steer you toward the success and unique personal satisfaction that creating a healthy, vibrant marine aquarium can bring.

CHAPTER 1

GETTING STARTED

*Planning Your System: Basic Choices
and Equipment for a First Marine Aquarium*

ETTING UP A SALTWATER AQUARIUM IS an exciting endeavor—creating an exotic marine world in miniature—and with some basic preparation and planning it should be neither confusing nor intimidating.

Although there are more steps here than in establishing a freshwater tank, many of the techniques and much of the equipment are the same and will be familiar to anyone with previous aquarium experience. (Getting one's sleeves wet with a freshwater aquarium is a traditional training exercise for most marine aquarists. For the intrepid and the quick learners, it is entirely possible to start right in with a basic saltwater system, but having some prior success in keeping less demanding freshwater fishes is a major asset.)

Left: a well-planned marine system can become a favorite focal point of the home. **Above:** surveying equipment at a local shop.

Beginning freshwater enthusiasts often begin on a whim—bringing home a goldfish bowl or 10-gallon tank with all the trimmings, including plants and fishes, with little or no forethought. With a marine tank, this would be absolute folly and something that no ethical aquarium shop would encourage. I urge you to spend some time thinking about the tank you want to create and to do some informal research before simply diving in.

PLANS & CHOICES

MAKING A PLAN IS THE LOGICAL START to setting up a new marine aquarium, but some people see this as a form of homework to be ignored or neglected. In truth, it ought to be fun, with a chance to look at your choices of livestock, equipment, and local aquarium purveyors without the pressure of making any buying decisions.

At this stage, you will start to identify the types of fish you really want to keep, then zero in on the equip-

TYPES OF FISHES TO BE KEPT?

- ❏ Mixed community fishes (docile to moderately aggressive species)
- ❏ Smaller, more docile species
- ❏ Larger, more aggressive species
- ❏ Species tank _____

TANK & STAND

Size of tank _____

Location of tank _____

Tank Material

- ❏ Glass
- ❏ Acrylic

Type of Stand

- ❏ Aquarium stand
- ❏ Existing desk, counter, or shelf
- ❏ Do-it-yourself unit
- ❏ Custom/other _____

Hood/Cover

- ❏ Glass cover
- ❏ Full hood
- ❏ Other _____

Tank Background

- ❏ Printed sheet
- ❏ Paint/other

LIGHTING

Type

- ❏ Single-strip fluorescent (not recommended)
- ❏ Double or twin-bulb fluorescent
- ❏ Compact fluorescent
- ❏ High-intensity fluorescent
- ❏ Other _____

Bulbs

- ❏ Full spectrum: number needed _____
- ❏ Blue actinic: number needed _____
- ❏ Other _____

BIOLOGICAL FILTRATION

Live Rock

- ❏ Cured
- ❏ Uncured

Type

- ❏ Base rock: pounds needed _____
- ❏ Reef rock: pounds needed _____
- ❏ Premium reef rock: pounds needed _____
- ❏ Other: _____
  pounds needed _____

Substrate (approximately ¼ to ½ pound per gallon)

- ❏ Dry coral sand: pounds needed_____
- ❏ Live sand (optional): pounds needed _____

MECHANICAL & CHEMICAL FILTRATION

Protein Skimmer

- ❏ Hang-on-tank type
- ❏ Countercurrent (airstone)
- ❏ Venturi
- ❏ Other type _____
- ❏ Air or water pump (if required) _____

Powerhead (total pumping capacity should be 5 to 10 times the volume of the tank per hour)

Number of powerheads needed _____

Model _____

Rating _____

Power Filter

- ❏ External canister type
- ❏ External hang-on-tank type
- ❏ Internal/submersible sponge type

OTHER EQUIPMENT/ELECTRICAL

- ❏ Heater(s) (2 to 3 watts/gallon recommended)
- ❏ Ground-fault interrupter (GFI)
- ❏ Power strip
- ❏ Lighting timer
- ❏ UV sterilizer (optional)

TESTING EQUIPMENT

Thermometer
- ❏ Internal
- ❏ External

Hydrometer
- ❏ Dip-and-read type
- ❏ Floating glass type

Saltwater Test Kit(s)
- ❏ Ammonia
- ❏ Nitrate
- ❏ Nitrite
- ❏ pH
- ❏ Alkalinity

WATER

Saltwater Source
- ❏ Natural seawater
- ❏ Aquarium salt mix _____
-     quantity needed _____

Water Treatment
- ❏ Dechlorinator/deaminator (for municipal tap water)
- ❏ Reverse osmosis unit (optional)
- ❏ Deionization unit (optional)
- ❏ Tap water purifying filter (optional)

QUARANTINE SETUP

- ❏ Small aquarium (10 to 20 gallons)
- ❏ Submersible sponge filter (with air pump or small powerhead)
- ❏ Heater
- ❏ Cover (light optional)
- ❏ Thermometer
- ❏ PVC pipe sections or fittings (as hiding places)

MISCELLANEOUS

- ❏ Saltwater mixing and storage vat(s)
- ❏ Utility bucket(s)
- ❏ Net
- ❏ Specimen box (for moving/acclimating fishes)
- ❏ Cleaning pad or wand (for glass or acrylic tank)
- ❏ Gravel vacuum with siphon hose
- ❏ Activated carbon (and media bag, if needed)
- ❏ Fish foods

ment that will meet your needs—and budget—and begin to plan the look and layout of the tank.

Thinking now about what will go into the aquarium and the overall design goes a long way toward determining how successful the tank will be in the long run. All too often, setting up a saltwater tank is an impulse decision. On several occasions, I have seen a new hobbyist walking out of a store with a bag of salt, a new tank, and several fish to put in it. This is not only completely irresponsible of the shop that allowed or encouraged this, but it is also cruel to the animals that have little or no chance of surviving. (It is also extremely shortsighted as a business practice, as most hobbyists who see all of their first fishes die soon after starting out are generally quick to find themselves another hobby.)

The Planning Checklist on these pages is included to assist you in making your choices. Many good aquarists keep a notebook or log, and this is a great time to start, making lists of species you like, equipment that has caught your eye, questions to ask, and prices quoted by different aquarium retailers in your area.

THE AQUARIUM SHOP

THE CHOICE OF AN AQUARIUM RETAIL SHOP will probably have as much impact on your success as a new marine fishkeeper as virtually any other decision you make. The right shop will not only provide healthy livestock and quality equipment, but the store personnel will also be important ongoing sources of help and information. Pick the wrong store and you may give yourself a triple handicap of borderline fishes, the wrong gear, and questionable or outdated advice.

The first thing that distinguishes a good store is how well informed the store's employees are and how well they can field questions from marine aquarists. Anyone thinking about investing in a new saltwater system ought to command some personal attention, and I would generally start at the top and try to talk to the owner or manager. (In a large store, you may want the manager or the senior salesperson of the marine department.)

The best stores generally have someone who was and hopefully still is an active aquarist. I like to ask the person waiting on me how long he or she has kept fishes and what types. Knowing that the person waiting on you is actively involved in the hobby is very reassuring. He or she may be interested in Rift Lake African freshwater fishes, but still ought to have a working knowledge of how to set up and maintain a saltwater tank. You definitely want and need someone who is up to date on the latest breakthroughs in the hobby in terms of equipment, techniques, and livestock.

I am always wary of shops where things are strictly business, and where anytime a problem or question arises the owner or staff immediately have some quick fix—usually a "just buy this" solution—to make it better. No matter what your problem, in the course of your hurried, one-minute discussion, these stores will immediately have an instant opinion and remedy for the situation. What the new aquarist really needs is someone who will listen, discuss the problem, and after assessing various options, come up with several solutions that may or may not require the purchase of something.

In many aquarium stores, the staff includes a number of young hobbyists who are eager to discuss their favorite aspects of aquarium keeping. These hobbyists can often provide tips, especially to the beginner, that are invaluable in saving time and money. On the other hand, some stores are staffed exclusively with minimum-wage teenagers or students with absolutely no experience or inclination toward keeping fishes. This type of shop is unlikely to be able to provide you with the service and information you will require when a problem arises. If at all possible, find a place that inspires confidence and where you can turn for honest advice.

Along with knowledgeable personnel, an aquarium shop ought to be clean, neat, and a pleasure to visit. This may seem superficial, but in my opinion, when a store is nicely kept and well organized, it generally indicates good overall management. It usually follows that the tanks are clean, the merchandise up to date, and the livestock properly handled and healthy.

"THINKING NOW ABOUT WHAT WILL GO INTO THE AQUARIUM AND THE OVERALL DESIGN GOES A LONG WAY IN DETERMINING HOW SUCCESSFUL THE TANK WILL BE IN THE LONG RUN. ALL TOO OFTEN, SETTING UP A SALTWATER TANK IS AN IMPULSE DECISION."

■ ■ ■

Check the displays of marine fishes and invertebrates: the tank glass should be clean inside and out with no salt buildup or algae obstructing the view of the inhabitants. There should be no dead or sick fishes in a tank where the animals are for sale. (When a tank contains sick fishes, some notice should be present stating that the inhabitants of that tank are not for sale or that they are being quarantined.) The tanks should be appealing to look at with no mulm (sunken debris) or excess food lying on the bottom.

The choice of fishes and invertebrates will also tell a great deal about a shop. Ideally, you will find the most-popular marine fishes, as well as some harder-to-find species of interest to more advanced aquarists. In smaller shops, especially outside major urban areas, the selection may be limited, but the fishes should always be well-cared for. (Any serious aquarium shop will be happy to special-order a species you want but don't find in stock.) A surefire icebreaker is to ask what fish species they recommend for new marine systems and to inquire about the types of live rock they offer.

As with livestock, better shops also contain a wide assortment of merchandise for all levels of hobbyists, with more than one brand of any type of product. (The trend at certain chains seems to be toward zero choice: "Acme" tanks, "Acme" lights, "Acme" filters, and "Acme" foods. How is one to compare price and quality if there is nothing with which to compare?) When asked about the tanks or protein skimmers, a good store should be able to show several brands and models and discuss the advantages and disadvantages of each. The merchandise should also be up to date and include some of the latest improvements in technology. (Determine if the shop caters to local reef keepers and regularly stocks soft and stony corals and cured live rock. If so, it is more likely to keep abreast of the latest innovations and information in the marine hobby.)

A good dealer should also be able to explain how various equipment works as well as how to repair it should the need arise. In this regard, better shops often maintain a workshop for repairing equipment as well as doing custom work like drilling tanks or building custom cabinets. These stores can help make an aquarium an integral part of a home or office by offering the resources to obtain customized tanks and stands and to assist you in modifying equipment to fit your space and needs. Finally, I would check the store's display of current aquarium books and magazines. This hobby is fueled by written information, and a forward-looking store will have the classic and current reference works to keep their customers well informed and motivated.

This dry-run tour of your local aquarium shops is an excellent way to survey the choice of fishes, the relative sizes and styles of aquariums and cabinetry, and the myriad choices of equipment. If possible, resist buying on this first investigative round of visits. Take the time to look, gather information, and plot your course of action.

THE BUDGET

AMONG THE MOST COMMON INQUIRIES a marine aquarist hears is, "What would it cost to set up one of these?" Given all the variables—size of tank, quality of the stand, selection of equipment, the way the aquarium is stocked, and where the materials are acquired—there is no easy answer. However, a tour of local aquarium sources should quickly provide a feeling for the approximate costs of a new marine tank, once you've narrowed the choices somewhat.

Marine specimens and systems are generally more expensive to buy, set up, and maintain than their typical freshwater counterparts. Synthetic salt mix is an ongoing cost that the marine aquarist must accept (unless a clean source of seawater is available nearby). However, much of the long-term expense commonly associated with saltwater aquariums has come, in the past, from the frequent need to replace fishes that have succumbed to poor water quality. In other words, the hobbyist who un-

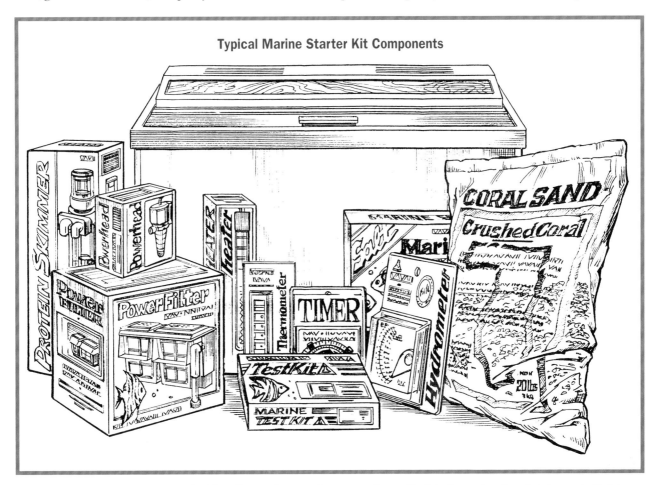

Typical Marine Starter Kit Components

All the basic nonliving purchases required for a first marine aquarium: many shops offer "starter package" savings to new hobbyists.

knowingly starts with a cheap, inadequate filter system will be paying the price of lost fishes within months.

The methods and setup for a saltwater fish tank described here will initially be somewhat more expensive than equipping an old-style undergravel system, but in the long run should be much less financially—and emotionally—draining. Using the accompanying advice on required equipment and supplies, you should be able to construct an approximate budget for the size and type of tank you plan to acquire using current prices from local retailers.

Obviously, the total price will be subject to a combination of a great many variables. In the end, you can make this as lavish or as frugal as your own tastes dictate and your pocketbook allows. The resourceful hobbyist can always find ways to cut costs, ferret out bargains, or otherwise achieve fine results by investing time rather than cash. The new hobbyist with an expansive budget will be delighted at the high-tech options and rare fishes available. However, keep in mind that success in keeping fishes alive and designing a healthy, beautiful tankscape has more to do with your methods than with the amount of money you spend.

Tank Size

Selecting the actual aquarium and its supporting equipment is one of the most engaging aspects of setting up a new system, but also one of the most confusing. The reason for this is that there are now so many different brands, pieces of equipment, and options from which to choose. But before you get into the smaller components and stickier choices, you need to decide on the main component: the tank.

The standard rule for setting up a saltwater tank is to get as big a tank as possible, both in terms of affordability and space. The tank itself is not the most expensive component of a saltwater setup, with a bigger tank generally not costing significantly more than the next size below it. Also, when you choose a bigger tank, the cost of the ancillary equipment does not increase in relation to the increase in the size of the tank. That is, if you go from a 20-gallon tank to a 40-gallon tank, you don't need two heaters and two protein skimmers, you only need to increase the wattage of the one heater and the size of the

one protein skimmer—neither of which will dramatically affect their cost.

There are several reasons why bigger tanks are better. First, a larger aquarium is more stable, in a number of ways, than a smaller tank. Temperature swings are moderated in larger tanks; if a heater malfunctions, a power failure occurs, or a heat wave strikes, it will take more time for the larger tank's temperature to shift to dangerous levels. Equally important, a larger tank is more biologically stable. If a fish or invertebrate dies unseen, it is much less likely to pollute the rest of the tank if there is a larger body of water to dilute the spike of toxic ammonia that can appear. A bigger tank is also more forgiving of typical beginner's problems such as overfeeding and overstocking and will reach a critical stage more slowly than a smaller tank. The tank itself cannot prevent ongoing mismanagement, but the extra margin of error provided by a larger tank allows more time for developing problems to be realized and corrected.

The other factor that often argues in favor of larger aquariums is the hobbyist's own desire to keep certain fishes. While many of the exceptionally colorful, smaller reef fishes can be comfortably housed in modest-sized tanks, others will quickly outgrow a beginner's tank. If your heart is absolutely set on having a 2-foot-long

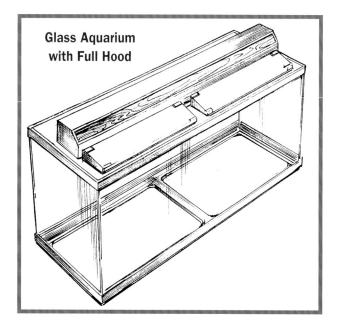

Glass Aquarium with Full Hood

Durable and affordable, a typical modern glass tank with lights and full hood is the starting point for most new marine setups. Many experts recommend a minimum tank size of 40 gallons.

gallon tank, which is mass-produced for the North American market and often available at an attractive price, with easily matched stand, lights, and other fixtures. Within the same family of 48-inch tanks, the choices of readily available volumes include 75 , 90, 110, 120, and 150 gallons, with a progressive increase in width and/or height. The usual, and in many ways most prudent, course is to start with something in the 40-to-50-gallon range, with a plan to move upward once your skills and confidence have grown.

I would counsel against any of the micro-sized plastic shelf tanks, or even small aquariums in the 10-to-20-gallon range, for marine fishes. Although small and cheap, they demand expert care and have a slim margin for error when it comes to stocking, feeding, and day-to-day maintenance (see Shoestring Startups, page 41).

TANK SHAPE

IN ADDITION TO CHOOSING A TANK of adequate volume, it is important to select one with the right shape—specifically, with as much surface area as possible. Simply put, it is prudent not to choose a tank that is significantly taller than it is wide. A lower, wider aquarium has several advantages over a taller, narrower tank with the same gallonage, especially for new aquarists.

First, a higher ratio of surface area to volume allows for greater gas exchange at the air/water interface. All other things being equal, a deep, narrow tank has a much greater chance of suffering poor oxygenation than a shallower, broader model. Taller tanks call for greater mechanical assistance (water- or air-pumping capacity) to keep the water well circulated and oxygenated. I am not placing a blanket condemnation on tall tanks, but they do demand properly sized powerheads and protein skimmers to compensate for the reduced surface area.

A wider tank also allows for a greater sense of front-to-back depth in the tank and this provides more room for a natural-looking aquascape as well as more potential hiding places for your fishes. The enhanced bottom area and places to seek cover can translate into increased security for the fishes and may help to reduce the stress of being in a captive environment. Tall "show-type" tanks have their place, especially in public or office settings where they will be viewed primarily from a standing po-

moray eel, a big lionfish, or one of the larger angelfishes or wrasses, a small aquarium simply won't do for long.

From personal experience, I would suggest that 40 gallons is a reasonable minimum size for a typical first marine tank. Provided that it is stocked intelligently, it can house a varied and interesting collection of livestock and is large enough to provide a reasonable level of thermal and chemical stability. A 40-gallon "breeder/low" tank is 36 inches in length, a common size for many necessary components, such as stands, hoods, and lights.

Moving up to the next standard length—48 inches, we find the 40-gallon "long" as well as the standard 55-

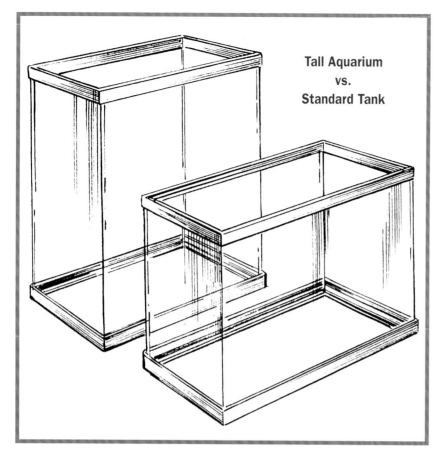

Tall Aquarium vs. Standard Tank

Lower is better: although appealing to some, tanks with tall configurations are more difficult—and more expensive—to keep well oxygenated and fit for marine fishes.

sition, but wider aquariums with greater "depth of field" or broader front-to-back bottom area can make for more interesting viewing from a sitting position—the usual arrangement for home systems.

Beginners, especially, will find a lower tank less expensive to equip properly, easier to set up and maintain, and more likely to sustain a healthy fish population. Many marine organisms are used to conditions with high oxygen content and good circulation, both of which are harder to provide in high or tall tanks.

Until recently, most aquariums built in the U.S. were tall and narrow, while those in Europe were generally shorter and wider. Fortunately this situation has changed, making it relatively easy to find a tank of just about any dimension. Bow-front aquariums, pentagons, corner units, L-shaped tanks, and many other configurations are available. All are perfectly acceptable, provided the height doesn't overwhelm the base, or footprint. (The hexagonal tanks available at most stores do not make very good

marine aquariums, being too tall and too hard to equip with skimmers, pumps, plumbing, and other necessary items.)

In summary, look for shallower aquariums sold as "standard," "long," "low," or "breeder." Think twice before buying a tank labeled "tall," "high," or "show."

GLASS TANKS

WHILE SIZE IS IMPORTANT, the composition of the tank presents a relatively simple decision for the new aquarist. Gone are the days when the only tanks available had stainless-steel frames and slate bottoms. Now just about all tanks are made almost entirely of glass or acrylic. A tank to house a saltwater system can be composed of either of these materials, and it is safe to say that this is almost never a "make or break" decision. Each choice has both positives and negatives, but the key factors for many people turn out to be price and aesthetics.

Tanks made from glass are widely available, with a large assortment of sizes, shapes, and trim options. Every pet store in the land has a selection of economical basic glass aquariums. The viewing panels are held together by silicone rubber sealant, with molded plastic frames to add stability. These are lighter, cheaper, and stronger than old-style fish tanks, and if handled with reasonable care will give years and years of leakproof service. Because they are so widely available in standard sizes, equipment to fit them, such as lighting hoods and covers, is usually easy to find.

While mass-produced glass aquariums in standard sizes are less expensive than acrylic models of comparable dimensions, there are a number of international manufacturers of premium glass tanks that add high-transmittance glazing, special sealants, custom trim, and many other options that can drive these glass tanks into the upper ranges of price and quality.

Acrylic Tanks

AQUARIUMS FORMED FROM ACRYLIC come in many shapes and sizes, some impossible to achieve with glass—at least on most aquarists' budgets. These tanks can have rounded corners, come in virtually seamless triangular configurations, and are even available as ovals or cylinders. The acrylic commonly used in aquariums has greater clarity and light transmittance than the glass in most tanks, although some observers feel the difference is negligible. Acrylic seams, which are less noticeable because of the absence of a thick bead of silicone, are stronger. (Keepers of large aquariums in earthquake zones sometimes choose acrylic tanks as better able to endure dramatic stresses.) The clean lines and lack of a plastic frame also make them more aesthetically appealing to some viewers and homeowners.

Acrylic tanks are much lighter than comparably sized glass units, making them easier to move and handle—especially in the larger sizes. Acrylic can also be drilled more readily than glass by the aquarist with standard power tools. (Drilling glass tanks is risky and voids any manufacturer's warranty. When possible, drilling should be done at the factory before assembly or by a glass-cutting professional. Many aquarium stores will arrange drilling of new tanks.) For more advanced aquarists wanting to custom-fit their own externally plumbed equipment, it is much easier with acrylic. Lastly, acrylic has significantly greater thermal insulating value—a factor in certain installations and a plus if the system is going to be kept chilled (below room temperature) to house other than tropical species.

Not all aquarium stores stock a full range of acrylic tanks, but most can order standard-sized models for quick delivery. Custom tanks—both glass and acrylic—will usually require a wait of 3 to 4 weeks, even longer with complicated designs.

A 175-gallon glass saltwater tank in a Florida home displays the architectural potential of well-designed aquarium systems.

Excellent aquarium location for viewing and stable conditions: away from direct sunlight and outside the path of constant human traffic.

Acrylic aquariums are more expensive than most of their glass competitors, although the disparity in price has been reduced in recent years. Acrylic can be scratched, both on the inside and outside of the viewing panels, by anything from sharp-edged decorations to cleaning implements. Many acrylic tanks have broad "lips" or sealed-on cover pieces with access ports; this feature adds strength but also restricts access during maintenance sessions. (Some aquarists like the semi-closed top, as it cuts down on evaporation and repels jumping fishes. Others find that it makes maintenance more of a chore.) The broad cover can frustrate your ability to add hang-on equipment, such as a skimmer, unless a utility slot has been cut in the top.

Boosters of glass tanks point out that the viewing panels can always be easily scraped clean with a utility razor, which makes for quick removal of even stubbornly attached algae. Acrylic-tank owners must exercise care never to use sharp metal blades or abrasive scrubbers on

their systems, but there are plastic scrapers for acrylic surfaces that do the same job as a razor on glass and are almost as effective.

In the end, glass and acrylic are largely equal in terms of their ability to house a collection of healthy marine fishes—the final decision will come down to cost, appearance, and personal preferences.

TANK LOCATION

AFTER CHOOSING THE SIZE AND TYPE of tank, the next decision is where to place it. Actually, size and location need to be decided simultaneously, as it is important that adequate room be provided for the aquarium. The tank should be located in an area where it can be readily viewed, but away from a constant rush of heavy activity. Keeping the tank away from busy human traffic is recommended because some fishes may become skittish and hide a large percentage of the time under such unsettling conditions.

The tank should be placed away from direct sunlight to prevent it from becoming overheated. For similar reasons, it should also be located away from drafty areas, heating or cooling vents, or an air conditioner.

One detail cannot be ignored: the tank must be near an adequate number of electrical outlets. Ideally, these should be above the tank to reduce the risk that saltwater, which is highly conductive, may come in contact with them. If the outlets are below the level of the tank, all cords can be arranged to create a "drip loop" for safety (see illustration, page 39). It should not be necessary to run long extension cords to power the tank's pumps, heater, and lights—which together require a constant and possibly substantial power draw.

To simplify planning and choosing a workable section of wall or counter, it helps to remember that the standard-sized aquariums selected by most new marine aquarists are usually 3 feet (91 cm) or 4 feet (122 cm) in length (see Standard Tank Sizes, page 25). These provide a range of volumes from 30 to 150 gallons.

In general, I wouldn't recommend going below 40 gallons or above 120 gallons for a first marine aquarium, as both larger and smaller volumes of water generally demand more care and expertise to maintain properly.

TANK STAND

ONCE ALL OF THESE CONSIDERATIONS have been taken into account, a stand for the tank needs to be selected. A sturdy counter, heavily built shelf, or desktop may serve the purpose, but for most aquariums, the best solution is a stand specifically designed to hold it. Saltwater is heavy—8.5 pounds (3.86 kg) per gallon. Even a modest 40-gallon glass tank filled with water, coral gravel, and rock can easily weigh 350 to 400 pounds (tank: approximately 55 pounds; water: approximately 255 pounds; rock and sand: 60 to 100 pounds).

Do not attempt to make do with a flimsy solution. A poorly constructed stand will tend to sag over time and may very well collapse. This is no trifling matter, especially for apartment dwellers. We all know how large a spill seems to come from a glass of water; imagine the mess from tipping over the equivalent of eight water coolers. To avoid disaster, be sure your aquarium has a good sturdy stand or unshakable surface on which to rest.

Water can damage untreated wood, and saltwater is notoriously corrosive. Appropriate materials for a stand or aquarium platform are sealed or treated wood and laminate-covered board. Several manufacturers of acrylic aquariums also offer coordinated acrylic-clad stands, which are impervious to water damage. I advise against the old-style wrought-iron stands, as these will rust quickly when exposed to saltwater.

For a small tank, the height of the stand and the space within the cabinet are not usually a problem. The prime consideration is in choosing a stand that will bring the tank to a height best suited to your usual viewing

Diversion for a home office, this modestly sized marine system houses a collection of hardy fishes and easy-to-keep corals.

Built-in marine aquarium graces a family room, offering an educational window into an exotic world of tropical reef life.

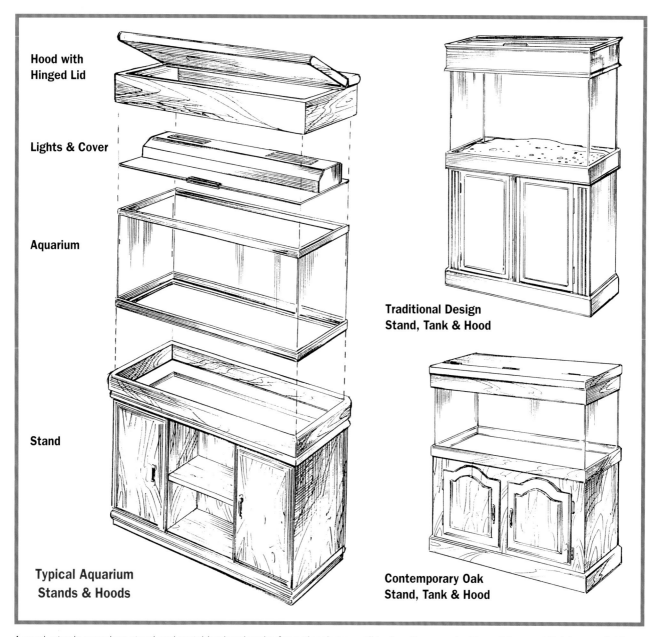

Hood with Hinged Lid

Lights & Cover

Aquarium

Stand

Typical Aquarium Stands & Hoods

Traditional Design Stand, Tank & Hood

Contemporary Oak Stand, Tank & Hood

A good, sturdy aquarium stand and matching hood make for a pleasing overall look, with many designs, styles, and finishes available.

position. A typical aquarium stand is made to provide an ideal view from a sitting position. Taller stands are for situations in which most observers will be standing.

For larger tanks, the height of the stand and the capacity of the cabinet require more planning. Advanced aquarists usually prefer to tuck filtration equipment underneath the tank, rather than within it. Often a sump (a separate water-handling tank), skimmer, pump, controller, and other gear must fit within the cabinet with convenient access for maintenance. If you are buying a tank with plans for future upgrades of this nature, be sure the cabinet you choose has adequate headroom, floor space, and wide-access doors.

If the stands on display at the aquarium shop don't appeal to you or match the decor of your home, ask about other choices. Some very attractive designs (traditional or modern in many finishes, ranging from washed oak and custom-stained hardwoods to high-tech laminates and textured paints) are readily available for many standard-sized aquariums. Some stores can also put you in touch with local cabinetmakers who have experience in creating tank stands and hoods or built-in aquarium units.

LIGHTING

MOST COMMON SPECIES of saltwater fishes are collected in shallow waters and are accustomed to good, strong lighting. For a simple marine aquarium that will house a collection of fishes, a lighting unit with two normal-wattage fluorescent light bulbs will not replicate the sun, but will be adequate and affordable.

I urge all new marine aquarists to shun incandescent bulbs, which create too much heat, and to avoid the cheap, single-bulb fluorescent fixtures, even for a first tank. While the latter is often standard equipment for new freshwater tanks, a single-bulb fluorescent light simply cannot show off marine fishes to their full advantage. This may be one of the reasons why some marine fishes look so vibrant in the store, but when taken home to a dimly lit aquarium appear disappointingly pale. One of the reasons we keep saltwater fishes is to enjoy their dazzling colors, but using only a single tube will surely negate them. Doubling the light makes a world of difference, giving a more natural appearance to the tank, allowing the culture of some attractive macroalgae, and contributing to the better health of your fishes.

Beyond the basic fluorescent fixtures, a large array of more expensive lighting choices can provide the intense illumination demanded by corals and other photosynthetic members of the reef community (not recommended for beginners). These include High Output (HO) and Very High Output (VHO) fluorescents, which require special ballasts and bulbs; metal halides, which must have special housings and ballasts; and some newer, high-intensity compact fluorescents.

HOOD

WHEN SELECTING a lighting fixture, the aquarist will have to choose among several hood and tank-cover options. The full hood, which both encloses the lights and covers the top of the aquarium, is a good choice if one recognizes that a common cause of fish death is specimens leaping out of an uncovered tank.

Full hoods greatly diminish the likelihood of fishes jumping out, but the downside is that most of these hoods are not designed to allow for the easy use of hang-on-the-tank equipment, such as a protein skimmer. If the system you have in mind includes hang-on equipment, be sure the hood will accommodate its presence or provide a space through which plumbing for the skimmer can flow. The other disadvantage of a full hood is that all of the heat produced within the tank can be trapped there. As a result, during the summer months when overheating can be a problem, it may be necessary not only to prop the hood open, but to add a fan to blow across the tank to keep it cool. (Hoods containing high-intensity fluorescent or metal halide bulbs are often equipped with small, silent fans to prevent overheating of the system.

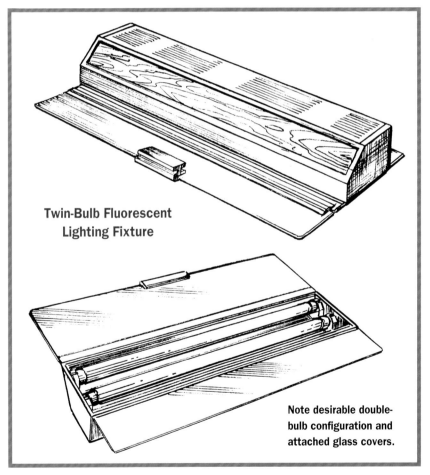

Twin-Bulb Fluorescent Lighting Fixture

Note desirable double-bulb configuration and attached glass covers.

A double-bulb fluorescent aquarium lighting fixture, often called a "strip light," will provide enhanced viewing pleasure and healthier conditions for livestock than a single-bulb light.

Reef aquarists are often guilty of keeping uncovered tanks, risking losses from jumping but coping with the greater danger of overheating from high-intensity lights.)

For safety's sake, most better hoods have a built-in glass or acrylic "lens," or sheet, between the lights and the water. Exposed bulbs tend to become encrusted with salt and occasionally may break—or even explode—if bumped or splashed with water while hot. Although such occurrences are rare, a lens helps reduce this hazard. At the same time, this clear sheet must be kept clean and free of salt buildup—otherwise light transmission will be dramatically reduced.

Generally, a full hood or strip light housing with attached, hinged glass lids makes good sense for a new marine tank. Tops, hoods, caps, or covers reduce evaporation, greatly reduce fish losses from jumping accidents, and help keep out dust, pets, and the fingers of curious children and other viewers.

FLUORESCENT BULBS

DOUBLE-BULB OR "TWIN" fluorescent light strips have become widely available in recent years. In addition to creating greater total brightness, they allow the mixing of different specialty bulbs to enhance the look of the aquarium.

Most fluorescent light strips and hoods sold to new aquarists come with bulbs designed to enhance freshwater plant growth. These are not necessarily the best choice for a saltwater fish tank. These freshwater bulbs cast a light that appears warm—yellowish or reddish—because the color they emit is high in the red spectrum. The only plus side to using these bulbs is that they will enhance any red or purple coloration in your fishes. (Never use "cool white" or "garden" bulbs over a marine aquarium.)

A better marine configuration for a twin-bulb hood

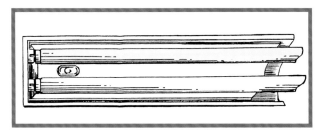

Many marine aquarists prefer to mix bulbs in their fixtures, often including both full-spectrum "white" and "blue actinic" bulbs.

would call for one full-spectrum "white" bulb and one "reef-type" or "blue actinic" bulb. The latter, available in a number of brands and variations, throws a bluish light that brings out the colors of many fishes. Viewers often find this light very pleasing when it is used in combination with a full-spectrum bulb.

A simple way to select bulbs is to choose the same bulbs as those used in the tanks at the main store where your marine fish are purchased, if you find their lighting pleasing. Most good aquarium stores use lighting that shows off their saltwater fishes to best advantage. Since this is the goal of a home saltwater tank, it makes sense to choose the same bulbs. An added advantage is that if you have the same lighting as your store, the appearance of the fishes should not change as soon as they are placed in their new home.

FILTRATION

TO COMPLETE THE LIST of essential equipment and materials, the aquarium will need a protein skimmer, one or more powerheads for circulation, a quantity of live rock, and, if desired, an external power filter or canister filter to remove particulate matter. All are discussed in detail in the next two chapters.

Filtration choices may prove to be the most interesting and lively part of visiting several aquarium shops in rapid succession. Ask each to show you their selection of skimmers, powerheads, external power filters, and live rock. This can be confusing or bewildering at first, but remember that you aren't trying to make a snap decision. I would survey the local market and then revisit the one or two best stores with follow-up questions once you've digested the first round and done some thinking and additional reading.

PROTEIN SKIMMER

WHAT IS PROTEIN SKIMMING and why does it improve water quality in a saltwater tank so dramatically? First, for those who have been involved with freshwater fishes, you are probably wondering why you have never heard of protein skimming. Simply put, a skimmer is almost useless on a freshwater tank. Protein skimming (or foam fractionation, as it is properly known) is a process that works much better in saltwater where enhanced surface tension allows the formation of the small bubbles that are the key to this filtration technique.

Briefly, a protein skimmer is an acrylic or PVC tube or box through which aquarium water is circulated. It is constantly infused or injected with fine air bubbles, either by means of a wooden airstone or a special air/water nozzle called a venturi. In either method, the mass of bubbles attracts dissolved wastes (proteins, fats, and other complex organic compounds) and floats them, along with other suspended detritus, to the surface of the skimmer, where the dark, wet effluent, or scum, is forced out into a collection cup for disposal.

A skimmer can remove eye-opening amounts of this vile waste from an aquarium—even one with apparently clean water. In years past, marine tanks were known to experience mysterious "sudden death syndrome" losses, which many believe can be traced to the slow accumulation of dissolved organic compounds in the water. A protein skimmer effectively removes these compounds, and

the mass die-off of fishes from unknown causes is almost unheard of in tanks with live rock and active skimming. In addition, the skimmer is a powerful tool for oxygenating the system water and driving off carbon dioxide, thus keeping the tank's pH level from dropping.

Small bubbles are crucial in forming a dense foam with a concentrated air/water interface. Protein skimming takes advantage of the fact that many compounds have two distinct ends—one that is hydrophobic (it repels water) and the other hydrophilic (it attracts water). These properties cause some of these compounds to become attracted to the surface of the bubbles where both of these attributes can be met. These so-called "surface-active" molecules are so strongly attracted to the air bubbles that they are floated up and out of the water column in the skimmer. A protein skimmer simply creates a large mass of small air bubbles in a confined space so that these surface-active molecules can become concentrated, collected, and subsequently removed.

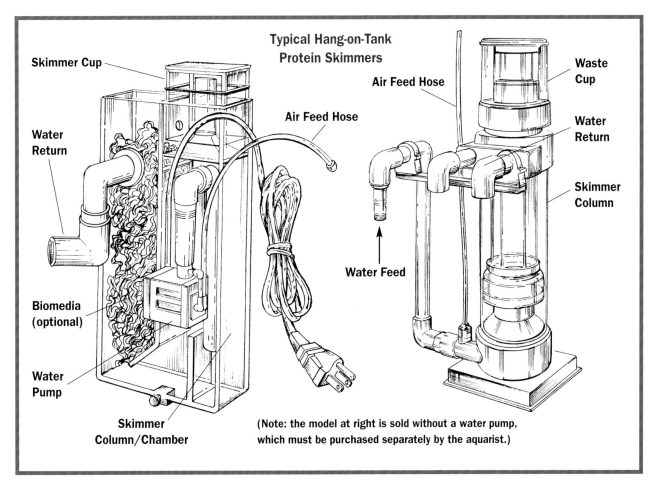

Typical Hang-on-Tank Protein Skimmers

Skimmer Cup

Water Return

Biomedia (optional)

Water Pump

Skimmer Column/Chamber

Air Feed Hose

Air Feed Hose

Water Feed

Waste Cup

Water Return

Skimmer Column

(Note: the model at right is sold without a water pump, which must be purchased separately by the aquarist.)

Easy to attach and maintain, an external hang-on-tank protein skimmer is a good choice for a simple marine aquarium setup.

Protein skimming can sound complex, but in practice it is actually quite simple. In most protein skimmers, small air bubbles are produced using either a wooden airstone or a venturi valve, which mixes air and water in a special nozzle that produces a constant flow of fine bubbles. These bubbles float upward, usually working their way through a moderate current of downward-moving aquarium water. Surface-active molecules (proteins, lipids, and other dissolved compounds in the water) collect on the bubbles and are carried to the surface of the water column in the skimmer.

Over time, foam collects at the top of this column, which narrows into a smaller tube or an inverted funnel to further concentrate the foam. This foam will climb up over the edge of the tube or funnel and collect in an effluent or scum cup from which it can be removed. The efficiency of the protein skimmer is determined not only by the amount of effluent removed but also by the density of the scum. In a well-functioning skimmer, the effluent can be the color and consistency of thick black coffee, with a strong, sulfurous odor.

The main factors affecting the efficiency of a protein skimmer are the size of the air bubbles and the contact time between the bubbles and the water. Smaller bubbles are better—they not only provide greater surface area, but they also rise at a slower rate than do larger bubbles. Wooden airstones like those used in most countercurrent skimmers produce extremely fine bubbles. Contact time is generally a function of the height and volume of the main skimmer chamber, where the air bubbles and water are mixed. For given rates of water flow and air injection, the taller and more voluminous the tube, the more efficient the skimmer. The slower the air bubbles rise and the greater the contact time, the greater the waste-collection efficiency. For most smaller home aquariums, the chamber should be approximately 18 to 24 inches tall and about 3 inches in diameter.

Most of the inexpensive protein skimmers designed to hang inside the tank are too short and narrow to work very effectively. In most instances, the skimmer is best located outside of the tank itself. Although not a hard-and-fast rule, bigger tends to be better in the choice of skimmers—in commercial and extraordinarily large installations some of the protein skimmers used are over 8 feet tall.

For a first aquarium, the simplest and most affordable truly effective skimmers hang on the back of the tank. An external hang-on-the-tank skimmer is usually fed with system water by a small powerhead pump immersed in the aquarium. After being fed through the skimming chamber or column, the skimmed water spills directly back into the tank. A number of good models are available through retailers who cater to marine aquarists. A good protein skimmer is an essential piece of equipment for all marine aquariums—not just reef tanks. It works full time to extract potentially toxic wastes from the aquarium and provides a site for very active gas exchange and oxygenation of the water.

You may notice "in-sump" skimmers that are attached to or placed in a sump—a separate water-handling and filtration tank that is often located below the main aquarium. Sumps are extremely useful for more advanced systems, but they do require more expertise to plumb and operate. Most newcomers probably ought to consider a sump a future investment, after they've started to master the operation of a more basic marine aquarium.

LIVE ROCK

AN ABSOLUTELY ESSENTIAL COMPONENT of any aquarium is a biological filter—a medium with a large surface area where beneficial microbes can grow and continually break down dissolved wastes. Live rock will be the workhorse of your biological filtration plan, being heavily colonized by beneficial microbes that feed on or break down dissolved wastes produced by fishes, decaying food, or other organic matter.

You will need to fill approximately one-third of the space within the tank with loosely arranged pieces of rock. Some hobbyists prefer to work with either less or more rock—from a quarter up to half of the available water space—depending on the aquascapes they are trying to create. As discussed at length in the next chapter, many choices of live rock are available, the primary ones being Atlantic aquacultured live rock (from Florida or the Gulf of Mexico) and Pacific rubble rock (from Fiji, Indonesia, the Marshall Islands, Tonga, Samoa, and other locations).

As a very rough rule of thumb, it will take approximately 1 pound of Pacific rock (which is lighter) or 1.5 to 2 pounds of Atlantic rock (which is more dense) per gallon of tank capacity. When pricing live rock, be sure to ask if it is "cured" or "uncured."

Uncured rock is much cheaper, but it is freshly imported and suffering the insults of collection and shipment, usually meaning that it has been out of the water (packed in damp newspaper in plastic bags or foam boxes) for at least a day and often much longer. Inevitably, uncured rock comes with dead or dying sponges, plants, crustaceans, mollusks, and other reef organisms—on the surface or deep within the rock. Curing it yourself means putting up with a week or more of strong odors while regularly cleaning or vacuuming the rock and changing its water.

Cured rock has been allowed to acclimate to captive conditions over a period of weeks (or months) in holding tanks. When acquired by the home aquarist, it should be free of dead or dying matter and have the clean, unmistakable smell of the sea or seashore. It is more expensive than uncured rock, but much less work and bother for a marine beginner.

Many aquarium shops have supplies of cured "base rock," which lacks much of the colorful encrusting coralline algae growth and other obvious life forms that reef aquarists treasure. This base rock can be a bargain and a perfectly good material for fish-only marine aquariums (tanks without sensitive invertebrates).

Ask to see the types of rock the store carries and other choices available by special order. Ask if the proprietor will cure such special-order rock for you (or at least hold it for a week while the worst die-off occurs).

Finally, be prepared for some surprised reactions. Many stores assume that only reef aquarists will be interested in live rock. A knowledgeable salesperson should appreciate your desire to set up a fish-only marine tank that utilizes live rock and skimming, rather than going through the usual undergravel filter stage.

EXTERNAL POWER FILTER

To help extract solid wastes from the aquarium water, an external power filter can be connected to the system. Actually, it may serve various functions, screening out suspended particles and detritus, housing activated carbon to adsorb dissolved wastes, perhaps serving as an auxiliary biological filter, and, by virtue of its water pump, adding to the tank's total circulation.

Two main types of external power filters are available: hang-on-the-tank and canister. Many hang-on types are rather toylike and designed for light use in small freshwater tanks. However, several heavier-duty units can be put to good use on starter marine systems, usually in the 50-gallon-and-under range.

Canister filters come in many configurations. They are often more powerful and have a greater capacity to hold filtration media than hang-on external filters. Be sure to ask how the different canister filters connect to the tank and how easy (or problematic) it is to stop, open,

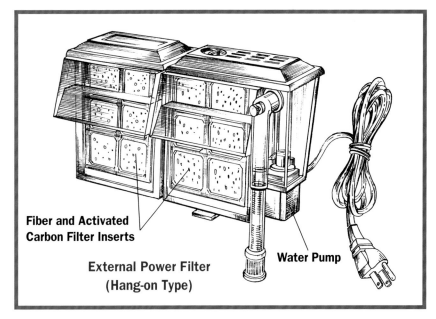

Fiber and Activated Carbon Filter Inserts

External Power Filter (Hang-on Type)

Water Pump

One of many types of external power filters designed to hang on the rear of the tank, providing mechanical waste removal, circulation, and a place to house activated carbon.

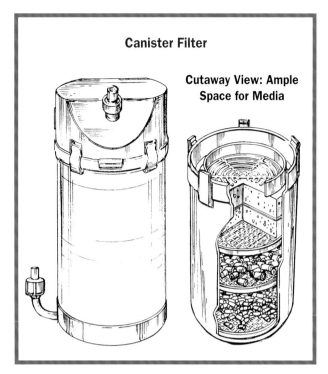

Canister Filter

Cutaway View: Ample Space for Media

A canister filter assists in removing particulate waste and provides space for activated carbon to extract dissolved pollutants.

clean, and restart them. A canister filter operates under pressure, and it must be shut down regularly for maintenance. The hang-on-the-tank power filters are usually open and can easily be serviced without losing the siphon and having to restart.

Other Filtration Options

SUBMERSIBLE, OR IN-TANK, POWER FILTERS, usually equipped with sponge media to screen suspended matter from the water, also provide some viable options. They come in various sizes (from puny to very powerful) and can be very handy for filtering a small aquarium or a quarantine tank if properly sized and maintained. In an established system, the sponge quickly becomes both a mechanical and biological filter, and must be rinsed regularly. The drawbacks of in-tank power filters are mostly cosmetic—many aquarists prefer to keep such equipment out of sight—but a good, reasonably powerful submersible power filter with a quantity of live rock and a protein skimmer can be a workable configuration.

Trickle filters, algae scrubbers, biological refugium filters, and other more advanced designs logically fall into the same category as sumps: interesting options for in-

termediate or advanced systems and aquarists.

Ultraviolet sterilizers are also gaining in popularity, allowing the aquarist to control or eliminate pathogenic organisms in the water without the use of chemicals. In brief, a flow of filtered water (perhaps that being returned from an external filtration canister) is passed through a tubular glass chamber where it is exposed to UV radiation that can kill free-floating microrganisms (both good and bad). Although hardly essential for most home aquariums, a UV sterilizer can help in systems where fishes or corals are plagued by certain pathogens. These units are relatively simple to install and use, but must be cleaned regularly and the bulbs replaced periodically, as specified by the manufacturer.

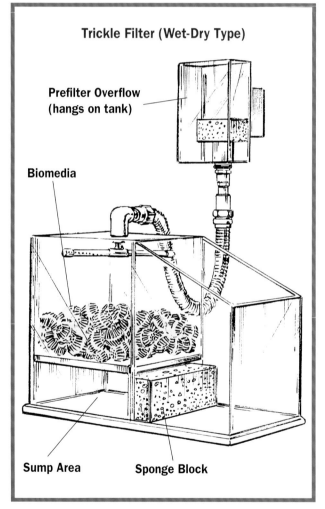

Trickle Filter (Wet-Dry Type)

Prefilter Overflow (hangs on tank)

Biomedia

Sump Area　　　**Sponge Block**

External sumps, usually located below the display tank, are highly useful for larger marine systems. Many hobbyists now remove the traditional biomedia (shown) and use the sump to feed the skimmer and to house other gear and filtration media.

POWERHEAD

POWERHEADS ARE A MODERN GIFT to the aquarium hobbyist, providing a simple, inexpensive way to boost water circulation. Most are submersible, with sealed motors, and are easily mounted to the back or side walls of the aquarium to produce steady or random currents.

Like heaters, powerheads for water movement need to be durable and reliable. For the most part, all powerheads look like little black boxes with nozzles. The best choices are time-tested, made by respected manufacturers, and usually slightly more expensive than the bargain units. When choosing among powerheads, look for the ease with which they can be taken apart. This is an important consideration, because powerheads must be cleaned regularly in order to work efficiently and not burn out prematurely. The motor also needs to be well sealed in epoxy, otherwise electricity can leak into your water and cause a shock.

A good powerhead must also have a method for eliminating the likelihood that fish will get pulled into the intake. In most instances, this means a strainer of some type. Unfortunately, for many powerheads this strainer is so small that the water intake is restricted, particularly over time as detritus accumulates on the strainer. The impeded water flow leads to overheating of the powerhead, decreasing the life of the unit. It also adds unnecessary heat to the tank. When selecting a powerhead, look for one with an oversized strainer or a choice of strainers that includes a large one.

How much powerhead capacity is necessary? In my opinion, the powerheads should turn over the water in the tank from 5 to 10 times per hour. In our example of a 40-gallon starter tank, therefore, we would place one or, better yet, two small powerheads with a total rated output of 200 to 400 gallons per hour. There is no scientific basis for this recommendation—it is simply the range of circulation volumes that I have seen work best in my tanks. If it seems excessive, consider that many reef aquarists now aim to have a total water circulation turn over of 20 times per hour. In a basic tank for fishes, this may be unnecessary, but the water movement should be strong enough to keep dirt and food suspended long enough to be trapped by the mechanical filter—but not so strong that the fish cannot move against it.

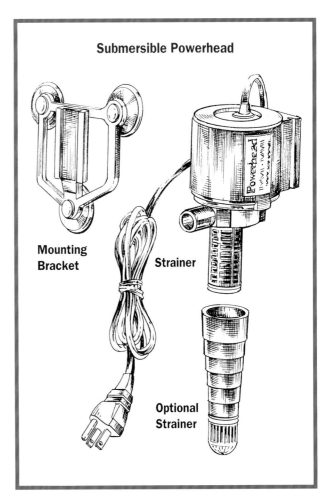

Submersible Powerhead

Mounting Bracket

Strainer

Optional Strainer

Every marine tank will benefit from having one or more powerheads in place to increase water movement and oxygenation.

HEATER

SINCE MOST MARINE FISHES come from tropical waters, it is advisable to keep the temperature between about 74 and 78 degrees F (23 and 26 degrees C). For most locations in North America, an electrical heater is necessary, particularly in the winter months. If the temperature in the room where your marine aquarium is to be kept ever drops below 74 degrees, a thermostatically controlled heater should be in place at all times.

Almost all heaters used today are self-contained, submersible units that have a built-in thermostat. Heaters are not particularly expensive, but they are prone to failure (leading to chilled or poached fish), so be sure to look for durability, reliability, and a well-established brand. Durability refers to how sturdy the unit is and how well it will take the small knocks and bumps that frequently occur. The heater should be prominently labeled as "submersible" and completely water tight. Even if mounted to the top edge of the tank, the chances of it falling in or getting splashed are very high, and you should be assured that water cannot seep inside.

Damaged or malfunctioning heaters have a history of causing aquarium accidents, and it is important to know that saltwater is a very good conductor of electricity. If a seal fails or the glass housing tube breaks, the damaged heater can deliver a strong or even fatal shock to the aquarist.

Reliability refers to how well the heater's output matches the temperature you set on the unit's control. That is, if you dial in a temperature of 75 degrees F, the average temperature in the tank should be 75 degrees F. It should be noted that there is usually a 2-degree F window (of permissible fluctuation) around the set temperature. This allows for the heater to come on less frequently than if the temperature window were only 1 degree and results in less wear and tear on the heater.

Experienced fishkeepers usually opt for the best submersible heavy-duty heaters available—this is one piece of equipment on which it never pays to skimp. Any helpful aquarium dealer will be happy to recommend a time-tested, reliable brand. A good-quality heater should last from 3 to 7 years before needing to be replaced. The main factor in a heater's long-term reliability is the quality and condition of its internal contacts, which can stick as the heater ages. If a heater's contacts (seen through the glass tube) show corrosion after a short period of use, expect problems with the unit and replace it.

The heater chosen should be sized at 2 to 3 watts per gallon to provide adequate heat. (Sunbelters may opt for the lower wattage, while aquarists in cold climates or in

houses that are kept very cool should aim for 3 watts, or more, per gallon to be safe.) My own preference is to undersize the heater as this lessens the risk of the unit malfunctioning and cooking the tank. As an alternative, you may want to install a pair of smaller heaters rather than a single large one. For example, a 50-gallon tank would usually call for a 100- or 150-watt heater, but two 50- or 75-watt units would do a better job, with smaller temperature swings and a reduced chance of one causing an overheating problem if its contacts ever became stuck in the "on" position.

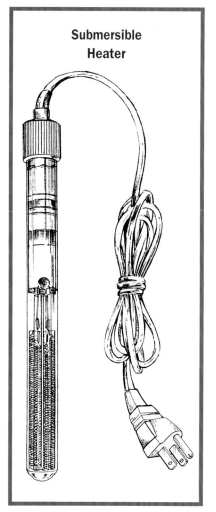

Submersible Heater

Thermostatically controlled submersible heaters allow the water to be kept safely within 2 degrees F of a set temperature.

THERMOMETER

ALONG WITH THE HEATER, a good-quality thermometer should also be used. There are several choices, including types that float in the tank or that stick on the outside glass. Electronic digital thermometers are very handy and easy to read, but are more expensive.

Whatever the design, the thermometer must start out giving accurate readings. This can readily be determined by simply looking at a side-by-side display of same-brand thermometers. Since they are all calibrated at the factory, they should all have the same reading in the same place at the same time. A group of reliable thermometers should consistently show the same temperature. Obviously, avoid the deviant ones—or a brand in which the readings vary from one thermometer to the next.

HYDROMETER

THIS DEVICE SHOWS THE SPECIFIC GRAVITY of water, a way to measure the salt content, or salinity (see page 48). Two affordable types of hydrometers are available to amateur aquarists, and both generally do an acceptable job of taking this important measurement.

A floating glass hydrometer—often combined with a thermometer—is placed in a tall flask of the water to be tested and a reading taken when the unit floats steadily at a certain level. (It is difficult to get a good reading by inserting a floating hydrometer directly into the tank.)

A box-type hydrometer is self-contained and used to scoop a small sample of water from the aquarium; a plastic float within the box rises to give a specific gravity reading.

In either case, the greater the salinity, the greater the buoyancy, and the higher the measuring device will float, yielding a higher specific gravity reading. The box-type tends to be more popular for three reasons: it is inexpensive, the readings can easily be taken from the front of the box, and it is more difficult to break. Various tests have reassured hobbyists that the ubiquitous SeaTest brand plastic box hydrometers do give acceptably accurate readings, better than some widely sold glass-bulb types. The box hydrometers need to be rinsed with freshwater between uses, and the bubbles need to be knocked off the buoyant arm during measurement. If this is not done, inaccurate readings can be shown.

In addition, the dip-and-read plastic box hydrometer is usually calibrated to read at a normal aquarium temperature (usually 75 degrees F/ 24 degrees C). Many glass hydrometers for scientific laboratories are standardized to read accurately at 59 degrees F, and a correction factor must be employed for aquarium use. If you opt for a floating glass hydrometer, try to find one marked "calibrated at 75 degrees F" that comes with an accompanying water-sample tube. The tube will allow easier, more accurate readings and may remind you not to leave the hydrometer bobbing in the tank, where—sooner or later—it will be broken.

THREE OTHER PIECES of equipment, all from the hardware or electrical supply store, should also be considered at this time: an electrical multi-outlet power strip, a ground-fault interrupter (GFI), and a timer.

The electrical strip will provide an adequate number of outlets necessary to set up just about any size tank. Of the types available, the most useful contain some outlets that are continuous flow and some that have on/off switches. This setup allows certain equipment, such as filters and powerheads, to be shut off during feeding or cleaning while the lights and protein skimmer can remain on. In addition, surge protection should be included to keep the equipment from being damaged should any electrical spikes occur. Avoid the metal-encased strips in

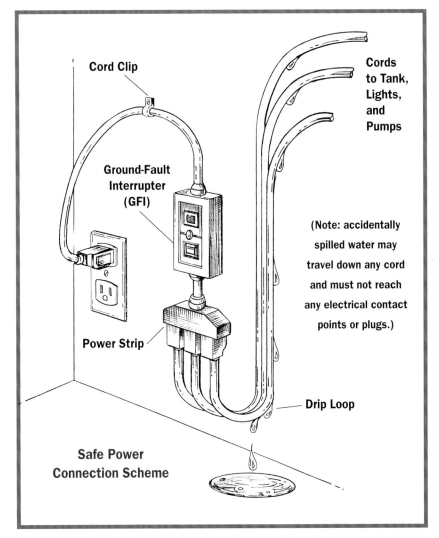

Cord Clip

Cords to Tank, Lights, and Pumps

Ground-Fault Interrupter (GFI)

(Note: accidentally spilled water may travel down any cord and must not reach any electrical contact points or plugs.)

Power Strip

Drip Loop

Safe Power Connection Scheme

Potentially dangerous (to humans and equipment) short circuits can be avoided by creating drip loops and running all electrical connections through a GFI safety device.

favor of noncorroding, nonconducting plastic units.

A ground-fault interrupter (GFI) is a highly desirable safety device that can detect "shorts" or ground faults and almost instantly cut the power to prevent serious shocks. An electrician or anyone handy with basic electrical wiring jobs can easily replace a standard, grounded receptacle with a ground-fault interrupter receptacle. Off-the-shelf GFI extension cords can provide the same protection without any need to rewire. These are not inexpensive, but they can prevent electrocution and are well worth the cost. Water and electricity can be a deadly combination, and having all your electrical devices fed through GFI-protected plugs is a precaution all informed aquarists ought to take.

TIMER

ON THE REEF, daylight lasts 12 hours per day, year round. Marine fishes have evolved over millions of years to live their lives by regular, predictable patterns of daylight and night. Even in a simple captive display, this regularized light/dark alternation should be mimicked.

The best way to make this cycle automatic and consistent is to use a household lighting or appliance timer to turn the lights on and off at the same time each day.

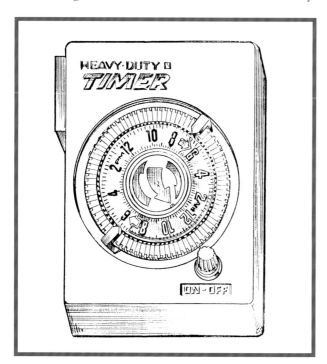

Marine life does best with a regular 12-hour period of lighting each day, and a simple timer ensures consistent on-off cycles.

These are available at all hardware stores, and they remove the burden from the aquarist to remember to do the switching manually. Erratic lighting patterns can interfere with your fishes' circadian biological rhythms, elevating their stress levels and interrupting their normal patterns of activity and feeding.

Since fishes are not used to sudden shifts from pitch blackness to bright light, the main aquarium lights should turn on after some other light has already come into the room. Fishes spooked by the sudden switching on of lights have a tendency to try to jump out of the tank or dash into objects. If your tank lights are set to come on during hours of darkness, a small auxiliary light may need to be placed on a timer to simulate a dawn period.

Similarly the tropical ocean is seldom pitch black at night, so I advise keeping a dim night light in the room with the aquarium. Since starting this practice, I've noticed less evidence of nocturnal aggression—nip marks and torn fins in the morning—among my fishes.

TEST KITS

TO THE NAKED EYE, two samples of saltwater can appear crystal clear and, for all intents and purposes, equal. Yet one can be a perfect medium for marine fishes while the other has deadly levels of ammonia or a very low pH—meaning the water is acidic and potentially damaging to living tissues and the animals' well-being.

We know the difference by using several elementary water tests, which come assembled as basic saltwater test kits. Usually included are tests for pH, ammonia, nitrite, and nitrate. These will all be especially useful in the early stages of operating a new aquarium. If selecting individual kits, rather than the more economical multiple test collection, it is usually a good idea to select kits from the same manufacturer. This is because most manufacturers use the same format from kit to kit, and once the directions are understood for one kit, it is usually not difficult to perform the same procedure with another. Also if a piece of any of the individual kits is lost or broken, the pieces from another kit can often be used, with the exception of reagents.

Any test kits chosen should be accurate and reliable. In addition, they should be easy to use not only in mixing or adding chemicals, but also in determining the differ-

If the cost of setting up a typical 40-to-50-gallon marine aquarium seems prohibitive, there are several alternatives for starting with a limited budget.

START SMALL

While larger tanks are easier to keep stable, a careful beginner who is willing to follow a few strict rules may be able to start with a 10- or 20-gallon aquarium.

With this size tank, everything will need to be done on a smaller scale. Just 10 to 15 pounds of live rock, 10 pounds of coral sand, and the smallest sizes of the other equipment will probably suffice. At minimum, you will need a power filter (external or submerged), along with a small powerhead, 25- or 50-watt heater, and light fixture. The tank must have a proper cover to cut down on evaporation, and the water level will have to be checked every day or two to prevent significant shifts in salinity. (Because of the smaller volume of water, any evaporation will more quickly affect the salinity.)

Religiously using activated carbon in the filter and doing weekly 10% water changes may allow you get by without a protein skimmer. (Change carbon monthly and add a skimmer as soon you can afford it.)

Stocking and feeding are often the biggest problems encountered with small tanks. You will have to accept a permanent limit of two to five small fishes. A good choice might be a pair of Ocellaris Clownfish (*Amphiprion ocellaris*) and a Royal Gramma (*Gramma loreto*) or Cherub Angelfish (*Centropyge argi*). (See page 84 for other fish options.). They will need to be fed with great care, as uneaten food can rapidly foul a small system. A few snails, herbivorous hermit crabs, and perhaps a cleaner shrimp will add interest and help maintain the tank.

The key to success will be to draw a mental line and simply say no to any further additions of fishes. Once the small community is established, it will be difficult to introduce any fishes without their being harassed mercilessly—or seriously upsetting the biological balance of the tank.

BUY USED EQUIPMENT

Another money-saving alternative is to buy used equipment. The classified ads often list tanks and related equipment for sale. Aquarium shops and societies will often direct hobbyists to used equipment. In addition they may also know of an aquarist who is moving from the area and wants to unload his or her tank. Many hobbyists are willing to sell their live rock and tanks at a discount rather than having to haul them across the country.

Be wary of taking on any used equipment, rock, or sand if the previous system was wiped out by disease or was subjected to heavy doses of copper and other remedies. The tank and gear may be cleaned and resurrected, but the live components of the biological filter may be contaminated and difficult to restore.

It is not absolutely necessary to purchase everything at once—some of the setup and acquisition of equipment and fishes can be done in stages.

TWO WARNINGS

1. If adding live rock in stages, cure it in a separate system first. Do not attempt to add fresh, uncured live rock to a display aquarium in batches. Once the tank is running and cycled, new additions of uncured live rock will be upsetting and may cause the death of fishes, invertebrates, and organisms on the rock itself.
2. Stock very lightly until you've established adequate circulation and biological filtration. Once these parameters are reached, the stocking of fishes can be done at whatever pace you choose, as long as new specimens are properly quarantined, acclimated, and introduced. (Add the most docile species first.)

JOIN A SOCIETY

If there is a local marine aquarium society in your area, start attending their meetings. Let people know you are trying to set up a marine system on a shoestring. Many aquarists have surplus equipment and livestock and you may find a motherlode of bargains and free advice. (With Internet access, you can also find a world of online aquarium information and contacts.)

ences in the values obtained. If the values are shown by differences in colors, the colors should be distinct when there are large differences in the values. If not, misinterpretation and a false reading can too often be the result.

Many aquarium stores now offer water-testing services, which give the aquarist a chance to observe how easy or difficult it is to use a specific test kit. If you see that a certain kit is difficult to use or has color changes that are hard to differentiate, it should not be purchased.

One of the advantages of choosing the same test kit as that used by your dealer is that your values should agree with theirs when you have them test the water. This can be a good way to check on whether or not you are performing the tests correctly and reading the results properly.

In addition, some dealers offer a guarantee or at least some compensation if a fish dies within 24 to 48 hours after it has been purchased—the condition being that the water in which the fish is placed is of good quality. If your store has this kind of policy, you may need to bring back both the dead fish and a water sample. Because test results sometimes vary significantly from one brand of kit to the next, it will help if your readings and those of the store are both obtained by the same measuring method.

Finally, you may want to choose a test kit brand for which refills are readily available from your retail store.

Salt

Synthetic sea salt will be required to convert tap water to a viable approximation of seawater. Be sure to acquire enough not only to fill the aquarium but to do a number of water changes. I would start with enough salt to mix up two to three times the volume of the aquarium itself. (Salt is more economical in the larger-quantity boxes and buckets. Once opened, however, salt exposed to damp air does tend to clump and become harder to mix. For the aquarist with a smaller tank, buying three 50-gallon bags of salt mix is probably a better idea than buying a single 150-gallon bag.)

Substrate

Sand, crushed coral, or other substrate will be needed to cover the bottom of the aquarium to a depth of ½ to 1 inch (1 to 2.5 cm). Be sure to ask for substrate of coral origin—reef sand, crushed coral, or aragonite—consisting of calcium carbonate. Shun playbox sand, dolomite, river gravel, or any of the artificially colored or coated substrates sold to freshwater hobbyists. Plan for about 3 to 5 pounds of sand per square foot of bottom or, very roughly, ¼ to ½ pound per gallon of tank volume.

Tank Background

Background material of some sort will be needed to give a finished look if the tank itself doesn't come with a colored back panel or darkened glass. In most cases, the back of a clear aquarium should be covered on the outside with opaque material or a coat of paint to give the aquascape a more realistic look and to hide any cords, hoses, or equipment behind the tank. Shades of blue or black are the most popular choices, and most aquarium shops offer printed waterproof paper or film material that they will cut to the length of the tank. (Some fishes will habitually "fight" with their own images, so mirror-backing can be a problem at times. Saltwater also tends to corrode the mirroring material.)

Tap Water Conditioner

A water-treatment fluid or tap water conditioner will be useful if your local tap water contains chlorine, chloramines, or heavy metals. Ask your store contact or a local aquarist about water conditions in the area to learn what water-treatment procedures, if any, other successful aquarists are using. If using a chemical additive to dechlorinate or dechloraminate your water, be sure to use a recommended brand from companies such as Kordon, Tetra, or Seachem. (Some inexpensive water-treatment formulas contain formaldehyde, which irritates the fishes' skin, causing it to exude a protective mucous layer. This method is cheaper than actually neutralizing the chlorine and chloramine, but obviously less desirable, with negative effects on biological filtration.)

Miscellany

A few sundry items remain to allow the smooth setup and establishment of a saltwater aquarium.

A specimen container, a medium-sized fishnet, a gravel vacuum with siphon tube, one or more plastic utility buckets, a container to mix and age saltwater, a quantity of activated carbon, and a cleaning pad or wand (for glass or acrylic, as the case may be) will round out the list of miscellaneous equipment and supplies needed.

At the same time, I strongly urge all new hobbyists to make the modest investment required to set up a quarantine tank. This simple, inexpensive system will repay its cost many times over by helping to make sure that any fishes introduced to your main tank are healthy. (See pages 113 to 115 for guidance on the setup and proper use of the quarantine tank.)

PRICE TAGS & STARTER KITS

PUT ALL THIS EQUIPMENT TOGETHER and the tally may come as a shock. Fortunately, most aquarium shops have "starter kits," designed to get newcomers quickly and easily into the hobby. If possible, you should take advantage of this opening discount, which is a store's way of starting a relationship with a customer who will probably return to buy fishes, salt, food, supplies—and, eventually, a bigger system if he or she becomes a dedicated aquarist.

Depending on who has assembled these packages, the price and choice of components may be very attractive or not at all appropriate. Beware of buying freshwater starter kits or packages that contain outdated, useless,

or unwanted equipment. Compare any such starter kit against the list of basic equipment in this chapter (see Planning Checklist, pages 20 to 21).

Many aquarium shops will be happy to work with a new saltwater customer to modify a starter package or to assemble a hand-selected choice of equipment, usually offering the equivalent of starter-package savings. If you decide to purchase most or all of your equipment and live rock (the core of your biological filter) from the same store, you ought to be able to strike a deal that would be considerably better than if you were to hunt down each piece from a different source.

One last note: supporting a good local retailer who is generous in providing free advice and a cost break on your first system is important. Many independent aquarium shops work hard at stocking healthy, net-caught fishes—including rare and hard-to-find species. Loyalty to a local store can repay you with priceless advice and help (including emergency calls and loaner equipment) when something bad happens—as well as a place for the housesitter to call when you are on vacation. Having a good aquarium shop within driving distance is a great advantage, ensuring that you have access to specialty marine goods and to healthy, desirable marine fishes and invertebrates.

CHAPTER 2

SALTWATER PRIMER

A Healthy Medium: Making It
Sparkling and Fit for Fishes

ABLUE ORB WHEN VIEWED FROM SPACE, the Earth bears a mantle of ocean water over more than 70% of its surface, leading some lovers of the sea to suggest that we really ought to be called the Saltwater Planet.

Although globally commonplace, seawater presents many unknown qualities to the average new marine aquarium owner. Some hobbyists find themselves becoming students of marine chemistry, while many others simply learn enough of the basics about tests and water-quality maintenance techniques to keep their systems and livestock thriving.

In either case, a basic knowledge of water conditions on coral reefs and how to replicate them in captive

Left: the pristine conditions of a tropical coral reef set very high standards for hobbyists trying to maintain proper water quality.
Above: South Seas Devil Damselfish, *Chrysiptera taupou*.

systems is extremely helpful to all marine aquarium owners. More than anything else, the quality of water you maintain in your tank will determine how well your fishes live, how much maintenance you will have to do, and, in the end, how much enjoyment you take from having a marine aquarium.

WATER CHEMISTRY

THE PIONEERS OF MARINE AQUARIUM KEEPING virtually all lived by the sea, where setting up a tank meant walking down to the shore with buckets in hand. Since the formulation of synthetic saltwater mixes in the 1950s and '60s, marine aquariums have moved inland and far from any need for easy access to natural seawater. Good synthetic mixes are even considered by many to be superior to the real thing in that they don't introduce parasites or pollutants but do offer enhanced buffering against pH shifts—not to mention convenience. If you

COMPOSITION OF SEAWATER

Major Ions		Minor Ions	
Chloride	19,000 mg/L	Bicarbonate	142 mg/L
Sodium	10,500 mg/L	Bromide	65 mg/L
Sulfate	2,600 mg/L	Borate	25 mg/L
Magnesium	1,350 mg/L	Strontium	8 mg/L
Calcium	400 mg/L	Silicate	8 mg/L
Potassium	380 mg/L		

Essential Trace Elements

Fluoride	Manganese
Iodine	Phosphorus
Zinc	Cobalt
Selenium	Nickel
Copper	Chromium
Tin	Vanadium
Iron	Molybdenum

Source: Aquarium Systems.

a mix is a relatively simple matter. All that is needed is a source of pure water and a good-quality synthetic mix.

In this chapter we will first discuss how to make up seawater, then explore the ways in which it normally degrades when populated with fishes in an aquarium. Finally, we will survey the equipment and approaches needed to keep your aquarium water quality high—the single most important factor in determining whether fishes live or die and whether film algae and other nuisances are constantly present or usually absent from your tank. Ultimately, the quality of the water in your system will determine how much success and pleasure you find as a marine aquarist.

SOURCE WATER: OCEAN

MARINE AQUARIUM OWNERS living near the coast often find that mixing up synthetic seawater is safer, more convenient, and perhaps even cheaper than collecting "free" ocean water. Natural seawater from shorelines near urban areas can bring unwanted pollutants, parasitic pests, and bacterial cultures that will bloom and die, causing aquarium conditions to decline rapidly.

Still, natural seawater is successfully used by marine fishkeepers around the world. Some aquarists simply adjust the water temperature, screen out any gross debris, and use untreated seawater in their systems. However, there is a long history of nasty pests, undesirable bacteria, and troublesome plankton (both plant and animal forms) coming in with raw ocean water.

The usual precautions to avoid importing problems with seawater include: filtering the water through very fine media, aging the water in the dark for about 2 weeks or longer, or treating the water with chlorine then filtering and dechlorinating it before use. Some hobbyists use a combination of these methods to ensure the safety of their collected ocean water supply.

SOURCE WATER: FRESH

WHEN MIXING UP your own synthetic seawater, a good source of freshwater is necessary—and this does not necessarily mean the tap water that you drink every day. Unfortunately, in far too many instances, municipal or well waters contain high concentrations of nitrate, phosphate, or heavy metals. National (EPA) guidelines allow up to

happen to live near a source of clean ocean water, by all means use it, taking reasonable care—collecting away from shoreline contaminants, doing filtration and aging before use—to prevent the introduction of disease-causing agents or pollutants. Most aquarists, however, will elect to purchase dried salt mix to be reconstituted with water from their home taps.

Synthetic seawater is not simply water with dissolved table salt (sodium chloride). (Place a marine fish in saltwater made with table salt and it will die.) Seawater is a complex medium that contains 6 major ions, 5 minor ions, and over 70 trace elements, including 14 that are considered essential to the health of aquatic organisms (see Composition of Seawater, above).

Fortunately, the composition of seawater is relatively constant around the world, and the average aquarist need not make special adjustments for the keeping of any particular species or group of fishes. (Freshwater aquarists must contend with very different sets of ideal temperatures, pH levels, and hardness readings for fishes from different waters.) Getting good artificial seawater from

10 mg/L of nitrate, for example, enough to cause headaches for aquarists. Some municipalities inject zinc orthophosphate into the water supply to prevent the leaching of copper or lead from home plumbing. Phosphates can feed algal blooms and be extremely harmful to some marine invertebrates.

If nitrate or phosphate levels are elevated in the freshwater added to correct for evaporation and in make-up water for water changes, these substances will be introduced continuously. As a result, their levels will slowly build, and the fishkeeper will see the consequences as nuisance algal blooms or ugly bacterial films.

Concentrations of heavy metals, such as copper, can have an even more deleterious effect because these elements are toxic to many forms of marine life. It should be noted that a home water-softening system is not the answer for removing heavy metals, as many of these systems dramatically change the sodium content of the water, which also will have a negative impact on marine life. To determine if there is a problem, you can contact your local water authority and they should provide you with a Water Quality Report listing the various levels of the compounds in your local water. (Hobbyists on wells can get their water analyzed by companies that sell and install water softeners and other water-treatment equipment. The service is often free, but they will naturally try to sell you water-conditioning equipment.)

If a better source for water is needed, there are several alternatives. Some aquarists simply buy purified water at either the grocery store or from the local pet shop. Many dealers now have purification systems in-house, so this is often another readily available source.

Aquarium shops also offer tap water purifying cartridges, which can be used to make batches of lower-cost deionized water at home. To supply larger quantities of pure water at pennies a gallon, it may be necessary to invest in either a reverse osmosis (RO) and/or deionization (DI) system. Without getting into specifics, these are usually compact canisters with filtration membranes and media that are able to remove a wide range of contaminants from freshwater. Reverse osmosis alone or in conjunction with deionization will be more than adequate for providing purified water for a saltwater aquarium. Many reef aquarists, as well dedicated freshwater hobbyists, swear by RO/DI water, but for a simple marine fish system, it may not be necessary unless the local water supply is compromised. (If a home water softener is present, the RO/DI system should be used to correct any imbalances it creates.)

SALT MIXES

IN ADDITION TO PURE WATER, a good-quality synthetic salt mix is also necessary. Not all sea salts are equal, and the cheap brands tend to give inconsistent results and may be deficient in certain essential components. Ask for a brand with a well-established reputation and avoid any bargain-basement mixes.

Newly prepared synthetic seawater is somewhat caustic and should be mixed up in advance of its introduction to an aquarium with livestock. Before being used for a water change, it should be aerated or circulated for at least a day in a separate utility bucket or clean plastic garbage pail to clarify (newly mixed saltwater is milky in appearance) and to allow time for the pH to settle down.

Dry synthetic salt itself should *never* be added directly to a tank stocked with fishes or invertebrates, even if the tank's salinity has dropped to a low level. Significant damage to the fishes' gills and body mucus can result, and the drastic change in specific gravity can be a shock to delicate invertebrates, if any are present.

Marine aquarium salt mixes provide a convenient method of creating synthetic seawater that is chemically balanced, well buffered, and capable of sustaining even delicate reef creatures.

SALINITY

SALTWATER WEIGHS MORE than an identical volume of freshwater and thus has greater density. Salinity is the measure of the total salts dissolved in water. Specific gravity (SG) is an indirect measure of the amount of salt present.

Among amateur aquarists, the terms salinity and specific gravity are used loosely and interchangeably, but there are no inexpensive test kits or devices that give true salinity readings. What we measure is specific gravity, using a hydrometer, and this is entirely satisfactory for managing an aquarium system.

The average density (salinity) of ocean water is 2.6% higher than pure water, and thus measures 1.026 with a hydrometer. The normal SG readings for most tanks range from 1.022 to 1.026. At these levels, most fishes, even those from the Red Sea, will do well. Fish-only aquariums may be run at the lower end of the range—1.020 to 1.023—without problems, but many keepers of corals and delicate invertebrates keep their tanks at SG levels close to that of natural seawater: from 1.024 to 1.026.

It should be noted that there is a relationship between temperature and specific gravity: cooler water is denser than warmer water. The importance of this is that many glass hydrometers for laboratories are calibrated at cooler temperatures (59 degrees F) and the readings change by 0.001 for every 7-degree F difference from the calibration temperature. Therefore, at temperatures above 59 degrees F, the observed readings on these hydrometers will be slightly lower than the expected value.

In practical terms, a beginning marine aquarium keeper is well advised to buy a hydrometer (either floating or box-type) that is temperature-corrected to read at 75 degrees F. If you always measure the SG of your system water and your replacement water at the same temperature—ideally at about 75 degrees F—there will be no need to worry about temperature correction. (Reef aquarists who keep demanding invertebrate organisms may want to use laboratory-grade thermometers, hydrometers, or refractometers to obtain more precise specific gravity and/or salinity values.)

PH

IN ADDITION TO SALINITY, there are two other chemical parameters that are important in marine aquariums: pH and alkalinity. Narrowly defined, pH is the ratio (expressed as a number between 0 and 14) of H^+ (hydrogen) ions to OH^- (hydroxide) ions. When both ions are in equal concentration in pure water, it has a pH of 7.0 and is said to be neutral. When there is an excess of H^+ ions, the water has a pH of less than 7.0 and is said to be acidic. Conversely, when the water has an excess of OH^- ions, it has a pH greater than 7.0 and is said to be basic, or alkaline.

Natural seawater has a pH range of 7.8 (deep ocean) to 8.4 (shallow reef areas). The goal in most saltwater aquariums is to have a pH from 8.1 to 8.4 (slightly alkaline). Over time, the pH in a saltwater system will tend to fall (that is, it will tend to move toward acidity). This is due for the most part to waste breakdown, detritus accumulation, and ongoing mineralization processes. In order to prevent the pH from dropping too low, it is necessary to maintain the system's alkalinity.

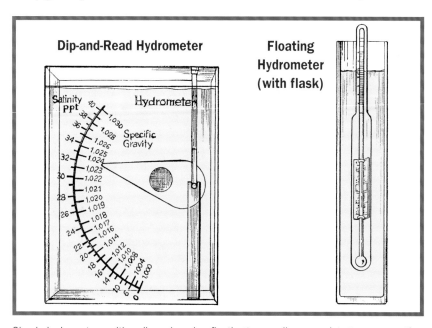

Dip-and-Read Hydrometer

Floating Hydrometer (with flask)

Simple hydrometers, either dip-and-read or floating-types, allow aquarists to measure the specific gravity of saltwater, a convenient method of estimating salinity (salt content).

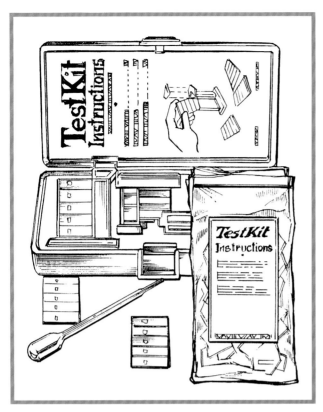

A typical basic saltwater test kit will provide tests for ammonia, nitrite, nitrate, and pH; an alkalinity test kit is also recommended.

ALKALINITY

ALKALINITY IS A MEASURE of the buffering capacity of seawater or the concentration of carbonates and bicarbonates present in the system. Buffering capacity refers to the ability of a body of water to resist pH lowering caused by acidification. (Acids are naturally generated in aquarium systems over time, causing a decline in buffering capacity.) Most scientists measure alkalinity in milliequivalents per liter (meq/L). The ideal range for a marine aquarium is 2.5 to 3.5 meq/L.

Many aquarists also use the dKH (degree Karbonate Hardness) scale, which is the (originally German) measure for carbonate hardness. The goal is to have a dKH between 7 and 10. (To convert dKH to meq/L, divide the dKH number by 2.8.)

At these alkalinity levels, even the death and decomposition of a large fish would not cause a marked lowering in the pH—although the ammonia rise could still pose a problem. Maintaining high alkalinity is a good way of preventing drastic pH drops.

In order to determine that these levels are within the proper range, pH and alkalinity test kits will need to be used. During the first 6 months of a new aquarium, these measures are generally not a problem. However, as the system water ages and if maintenance is lax or inadequate, these values may begin to fall. Therefore, after about 6 months, testing for pH and alkalinity should begin, if only on a monthly basis. In order to prevent a drop in pH and to maintain the alkalinity (buffering capacity) of your aquarium water, it may be necessary to add buffer and to increase the amount or frequency of water changes.

One other aspect of water chemistry that needs to be addressed is stability. Owing to its immense size, the ocean, for the most part, is a very stable environment. As a result, fishes are not accustomed to dramatic changes of pH. Even a pH as low as 7.9 may not be deleterious to captive fishes that have lived in that environment and have gradually experienced a decline from 8.3 to 7.9. But a new fish dropped into this water would probably not survive. Therefore even if there is a sudden realization that the tank's chemical parameters are inappropriate, if the tank is doing well, changes to bring the levels to their proper place should only be done gradually over several days or weeks. Otherwise the tank's inhabitants that were thriving could be severely stressed or even fatally shocked. Except for emergency situations, most changes in water chemistry are best done slowly.

TEMPERATURE

THERE IS A DIRECT RELATIONSHIP between temperature and pH. Actually there is a relationship between just about everything that goes on in a saltwater tank and temperature. Since all of the inhabitants are cold-blooded (unable to control their own body temperatures), they are dependent on the temperature of the surrounding environment. The fish's metabolism, the rate of waste decomposition, the metabolism of bacteria and other nonvertebrate life are all dependent on the temperature.

Most of the inhabitants of a saltwater aquarium will do well with consistent temperatures of between 72 and 82 degrees F (22 and 28 degrees C), with the optimum range being between 74 and 78 degrees F (23 and 26 degrees C). Generally speaking, the lower average temperatures are better for most tanks. Not only does cooler water hold more oxygen, but lower temperatures also result in slower metabolism. Fishes will tend to eat less, grow slower, and live longer. Since most bad things—disease outbreaks, death, and decomposition—happen fast, if we can slow the process down we may be able to remedy the problem before it gets out of hand. While higher temperatures may be desirable for breeding or getting the maximum growth from young fishes or corals, most aquarists will find that a temperature closer to 75 degrees F, rather than 80 or higher, makes for a healthier system.

Provided the changes are gradual, most reef fishes can tolerate brief episodes in which the temperature ranges down to about 68 degrees F or up to about 86, but in general the aquarist should be on the alert if the system drifts out of the 70-to-80-degree F zone. Once again, keep things as stable as possible and make all changes gradually. If the tank's temperature rises to 86 degrees F over a period of hours, it should not be brought back down to 76 in 15 minutes. It must be reduced, but slowly. The most common aftereffect of sudden temperature shifts (if they don't kill your fishes outright) is the onset of disease, often triggered by stress.

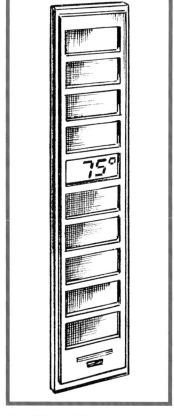

With 72°F to 82°F as a safe range for water temperature, 75°F is a recommended day-to-day target.

WATER MOVEMENT

ONE OF THE OBVIOUS EXPLANATIONS for the ocean's great stability and chemical uniformity—compared to bodies of freshwater—is its constant circulation. Wave action, tides, and currents all help to distribute both good and bad elements across large volumes of water so that nothing becomes too concentrated in any one spot. Fish wastes, for example, are rapidly dispersed (or consumed), and reef waters normally show zero readings when tested for such common aquarium pollutants as ammonia, nitrite, nitrate, and phosphate. Heated surface waters, outside the lagoon or inner reef, are constantly mixed with cooler underlying waters, creating thermal, as well as

chemical, stability to rather surprising depths on and around coral reefs. While freshwater lakes tend to stratify and be considerably cooler at greater depths, the prevailing temperature on a reef may extend down some 150 feet (45 m) or more, with temperatures in the high 70s even down to 300 feet (90 m).

Reef fishes have evolved to deal with almost constant water motion. Unfortunately, in many closed systems, water movement is either an afterthought or entirely forgotten. As a result, many marine aquariums more closely resemble a pond rather than the ocean in terms of the amount of water motion. Part of this stems from the adaptation of old freshwater aquarium equipment, such as the undergravel filter, to saltwater use. These filters tend to have relatively modest abilities to circulate aquarium water in the best of situations, and then typically decline further in performance as the filtration medium becomes clogged with detritus.

With what we know now, vigorous water movement is not a luxury but rather a necessity for the well-being of the fishes in a captive marine system. Strong water movement helps to prevent dead spots from forming within the tank and keeps uneaten food and detritus suspended in the water column so that it can be filtered out. Brisk circulation triggers natural feeding reactions in fishes, as frozen and dried foods are moved by the currents and thus mimic the behavior of wild prey items. Active water movement will also keep the biological filtration efficiency of live rock high, bringing dissolved wastes and oxygenated water quickly to the nitrifying bacterial populations. Lastly, strong water movement keeps the fish swimming, which, like exercise for humans, builds and maintains fitness. (Notice the big, overfed, old specimens in the quiet tanks in some long-established public aquariums. Some are so fat and misshapen as to barely resemble members of their own species in the wild.)

In a smaller closed system, adequate water movement can easily be provided by the returns from a protein skimmer and external power filter, along with direct in-the-tank output from one or more powerheads. These small submersible water pumps direct appreciable flows of water in a constant stream. For optimum effect, I like to use at least two of these powerheads in any tank—a pair of smaller pumps being better than a single larger one. The pair should be placed on opposite ends of the tank and their flows directed either toward each other or in an X pattern. In this way, maximum turbulence and shifting flow patterns can be achieved. (Reef aquarists often invest in "wavemakers" or timing switches that alternate or randomize the flows of two or more powerheads. Consider this a future investment.)

Aquarium powerheads come in a range of sizes, with ratings based on the volume of water they move under ideal conditions. The powerheads—along with the water moved by external filter pumps—should have a combined output rating that is from 5 to 10 times the volume of the tank. (A 50-gallon aquarium, for example, should have a total circulation turnover of at least 250 to 500 gallons per hour. Two small powerheads rated at 150 to 250 gallons per hour each would do the job nicely, augmented by the less vigorous return from a protein skimmer.)

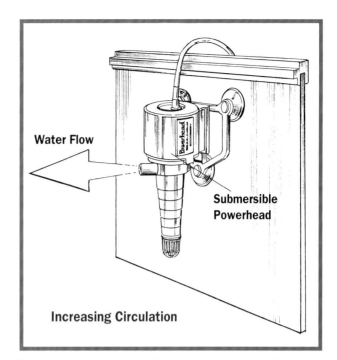

Inadequate water circulation is a common aquarium problem but is easily remedied by adding a small powerhead pump or two.

NUTRIENT CYCLING

To PUT IT SIMPLY, all organisms produce waste and many of these waste products can be toxic if allowed to circulate freely in the environment. Fishes live in an aqueous environment, and their waste products are released as dissolved ammonia (excreted through the gills) or as solid and semisolid wastes, some of which tend to dissolve quickly in the water column.

In the wild, this is not a problem because of several factors. First, currents and the movement of the water widely distribute the waste and keep it from accumulating in any one spot. Because of the large volume of water present, this waste becomes diluted even further over time. Large populations of bacteria are also present on virtually every ocean surface, consuming or converting much of the dissolved waste material into less toxic forms. Filter-feeding organisms also catch much of the suspended detritus, and myriad invertebrates—such as corals, clams, mollusks, and algae—also feed on dissolved nutrients. (Among the fishes and invertebrates are many "detritivores" that greedily consume solid fish waste.) This array of organisms that rapidly recycle both dissolved and particulate wastes explains the paradox of the biologically packed reef habitat existing in nutrient-starved waters.

This situation changes dramatically in a captive system. The volume of water is much smaller and the ratio of fish mass to water volume is exponentially higher. In addition to being overstocked, many fish tanks are also overfed. While this can often be overcome in a freshwater tank, in a saltwater system, because of the differences in chemistry, it cannot. This is because in most freshwater systems, where the pH is less than 7.0, the nitrogenous waste occurs primarily as ammonium. At this pH, ammonium is relatively nontoxic and bacteria in the tank quickly break it down into less toxic compounds like nitrite and nitrate. In the marine aquarium, where the pH should always be over 8.0, fishes excrete ammonia through their gills, and ammonium from other sources can also be transformed to ammonia. Because ammonia is toxic to most marine organisms even at low concentrations, it must somehow be detoxified—and quickly.

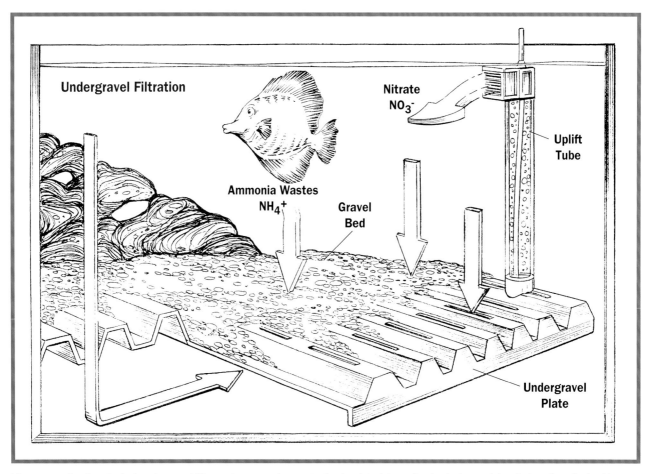

Nitrogen cycling in a typical undergravel filter setup: aquarium water is circulated through a bed of gravel that is heavily colonized by bacteria, which convert toxic ammonia first to nitrite, which is less toxic, then to nitrate, which is tolerated by marine fishes.

BIOLOGICAL FILTRATION

IN ORDER TO PREVENT even small amounts of ammonia from persisting in the tank, it is necessary to establish some means of breaking it down as rapidly as possible. Fortunately, there are bacteria that thrive on various forms of nitrogenous waste, both fueling their own existence and detoxifying the tank's ammonia. This process is known as nitrification, or biological filtration—wherein living microbes attack and render toxic ammonia harmless.

Thus the crucial element for having a successful saltwater aquarium is to establish populations of the proper bacteria. The conversion of ammonia into nitrate is a two-step process involving at least two different types of bacteria. First, nitrifying bacteria (usually described as *Nitrosomonas* species) convert ammonia into nitrite, which is still somewhat toxic to marine life. Then, a second type of bacteria (traditionally thought to be *Ni-trobacter* species) that grow in conjunction with the first, oxidize nitrite into nitrate, which is essentially harmless to marine life when present in low or moderate concentrations.

Early marine tanks tended to be death traps for fishes. They were equipped with tiny air-driven filters, borrowed from the freshwater hobby, that were vastly underpowered and had too little area for bacterial growth. In these tanks, significant problems were encountered because the bare decor, poor circulation, and low oxygen levels provided unsatisfactory conditions for the development of healthy populations of nitrifying bacteria. When fish died, tanks were often torn down and disinfected, thereby eliminating any beneficial bacterial cultures that may have been forming. Fortunately, our understanding of the role of biological filtration and methods for ensuring that it takes place efficiently in the marine aquarium have improved greatly in recent decades.

Undergravel Filtration

BIOLOGICAL FILTRATION IN THE AQUARIUM may sound a bit mysterious, but from a practical standpoint, all that is really necessary is a bacterial culture, a place for it to live and reproduce, an ammonia source, and time. When these components are utilized properly, a marine tank will "cycle" itself and have a full complement of useful bacteria develop pretty much on its own.

Beginning in the 1960s, undergravel filter plates covered with sand dramatically increased the amount of media available for bacterial growth, as well as the water movement and oxygen levels in the tank. Water in the aquarium was continuously drawn down through the sand under the plastic filter plate, and lifted by air in riser tubes to be returned to the tank (see illustration at left). Initial survival rates for fishes jumped in systems with undergravel filters, and in the decades since, most new beginner aquariums in North America have been set up using this simple technology. Unfortunately, there are serious shortcomings with the undergravel system that reduce the chances of long-term success.

In order for the undergravel system to work, the bacteria need well-oxygenated water to flow over them. However, in an undergravel filter, this continuous flow of tank water also carries detritus (uneaten food, solid waste, dead algae, etc.), which is caught in the substrate, clogging the channels through which the aquarium water is trying to flow. As a result, the efficiency of the filter deteriorates over time. In a worst-case scenario, areas in the sand and beneath the undergravel plate become deprived of oxygen (anaerobic) and highly toxic compounds, such as hydrogen sulfide, may form and can wipe out the entire tank.

In order to reduce the chances of this happening, proponents of undergravel filters advocate stirring the gravel and removing detritus during water changes. Unfortunately, even when this is practiced, it is still usually necessary to break down the entire tank due to the amount of detritus that accumulates under the plate itself. Breaking down means removing all of the contents of the tank, including the gravel and the filter plate, so that accumulated debris can be removed. This generally needs to be done every 12 to 18 months, depending on the tank's bioload.

Another drawback of this system is that only a minimum of aquascaping material can be placed on the substrate above the undergravel filter. Dead spots can quickly develop in areas with too much coverage, and this will result in the tank needing to be broken down more frequently.

To keep an undergravel sand bed exposed to active water flow, only a few coral skeletons or fiberglass or resin coral replicas are typically used for decoration. Not only is the use of dead coral skeletons environmentally questionable, but it is hardly a natural, stress-free habitat for the tank's inhabitants. A few bleached white corals sitting atop white sand provide few hiding places for the fishes and also cause the coloration of many fishes to fade. (Marine fishes have amazing abilities to adapt their coloration to their surroundings. In an unnaturally white aquascape, they tend to shift to lighter, less attractive colors.) In addition, the overall appearance of an aquarium decorated with dead coral is not very realistic or visually appealing, especially to anyone who has ever seen what a live coral reef in the wild actually looks like.

> "A FEW BLEACHED WHITE CORALS SITTING ATOP WHITE SAND PROVIDE FEW HIDING PLACES FOR THE FISHES AND ALSO CAUSE THE COLORATION OF MANY FISHES TO FADE. MARINE FISHES HAVE AMAZING ABILITIES TO ADAPT THEIR COLORATION TO THEIR SURROUNDINGS. IN AN UNNATURALLY WHITE AQUASCAPE, THEY TEND TO SHIFT TO LIGHTER, LESS ATTRACTIVE COLORS."
>
> ■ ■ ■

Trickle Filters

OTHER BIOLOGICAL FILTRATION DEVICES have appeared to overcome the limitations of the undergravel filter. These include the so-called wet-dry or trickle filters that helped spawn the reef aquarium hobby in the 1980s. These filters are still popular with many hobbyists, and they typically contain "biomedia"—ranging from coarse coral rubble to plastic Bio-Balls, grids, and synthetic fabric mesh—on which bacterial cultures can proliferate. This media is usually contained in a separate tank or sump, often below the display aquarium. Here, well-oxygenated water from the system is continuously dripped or sprayed over the mass of biomedia before being collected in the bottom of the sump and pumped back to the aquarium.

Trickle filters can be credited with advancing the marine hobby by increasing circulation substantially, adding to the water volume of the system being kept, and allowing detritus to be mechanically screened out before it reaches the biomedia. Such filters are extremely efficient at breaking down ammonia.

A major downside of most trickle filters, as well as undergravel filters, is that they tend to produce nitrate as an end product. While not toxic to fishes, even in rather high concentrations, nitrate does fuel the growth of nuisance algae and is not well tolerated by some invertebrates.

LIVE ROCK AS A BIOFILTER

THANKFULLY, WE NOW HAVE A BETTER and more realistic-looking approach to biological filtration and marine fishkeeping. Taking a lesson from all that has been learned about reef tanks over the past decade, we have seen that live rock makes a perfect biological filter. It accommodates huge populations of bacteria, performs steadily with little maintenance, provides appropriate shelter for fishes, and makes the most natural aquascaping material possible.

Live rock has revolutionized the keeping reef aquariums by acting as a complete biological filter. It can host tremendous quantities of nitrifying bacteria that will detoxify the dissolved nitrogenous wastes in an aquarium. Unlike most active biological filtration devices, live rock can also act as a site where denitrification (the conversion of nitrate to harmless nitrogen gas) can take place in anaerobic or very low oxygen conditions.

Traditionally, we have tried to limit the formation of these anaerobic (oxygen-free) areas in marine aquariums. Fortunately, live rock offers an effective method of preventing nitrate accumulation, by allowing anaerobic processes to take place deep within the rock, but with none of the risks or maintenance challenges typically associated with other anaerobic filters.

Since the live rock's surfaces and inner spaces that house bacteria should not become clogged or closed over time—as normally occurs with undergravel filter beds—a tank using live rock should not need to be broken down for cleaning. Many such systems have been running for more than 10 years without an overhaul, and in fact seem to perform better, rather than worse, as time passes.

Without the highly disruptive changes of a complete tank teardown, there is less stress on the tank's inhabitants, and there is no longer a need to regenerate adequate bacterial populations after a major cleaning session. Live rock does accumulate some detritus, but this can easily be blown free by a squirt from a turkey baster or the current from a small, hand-held powerhead (to be caught subsequently by the mechanical filter)—or it can be siphoned out during routine water changes. For the most part, live rock is the ultimate low-maintenance aquascaping material, requiring no handling, scrubbing, or special care once it is in place.

Beyond superior filtration and ease of care, live rock has other benefits. To most observers, live rock makes for a more authentic, natural-looking tank than dead coral skeletons. (The overcollection of large corals for souvenirs and decorative purposes is a problem in some areas, while the taking of live rock from rubble zones has a minimal impact on the reef.) In addition, bleached coral skeletons—a "look" that was popular in the earlier days of marine aquarium keeping—become unsightly rather quickly with the growth of green algae and are a nuisance to keep clean. This part of the look helped drive people away from the keeping of marine fishes.

Tanks using the live rock method are not only more visually pleasing, but the tank's inhabitants seem to be less stressed and jittery than when they are housed with the typical collection of dead coral skeletons. In addition, live rock also provides many fishes with a source of live foods. Algae tends to grow readily on the surface where herbivores will constantly graze. (Minor algae growth on live rock blends easily into the reef scene, while green splotches on stark, bleached corals seem to signal a lack of maintenance.) Also various other animals like worms and copepods live and reproduce in the rock, and these creatures are a welcome dietary addition for many species of reef fishes. These other attributes of live rock and its handling will be discussed more fully in the following chapter.

MECHANICAL FILTRATION

IN ADDITION TO AN ACTIVE BIOLOGICAL FILTER, two other types of filtration are commonly utilized in a well-running marine aquarium: mechanical filtration (to remove particulate matter) and chemical filtration (to remove dissolved compounds).

Unlike biological filtration, which is a complex chain of events invisible to the naked eye, mechanical filtration is relatively simple. As its name implies, mechanical filtration is the removal of waste by physically trapping suspended solids. In most instances, the tank's water flows through a piece of sponge or fiber where suspended wastes (fish feces, uneaten food, dead algae, and other debris and detritus) are caught and held. This works well in the short term, but over time, this trap—if not cleaned—can become a mass of decaying wastes.

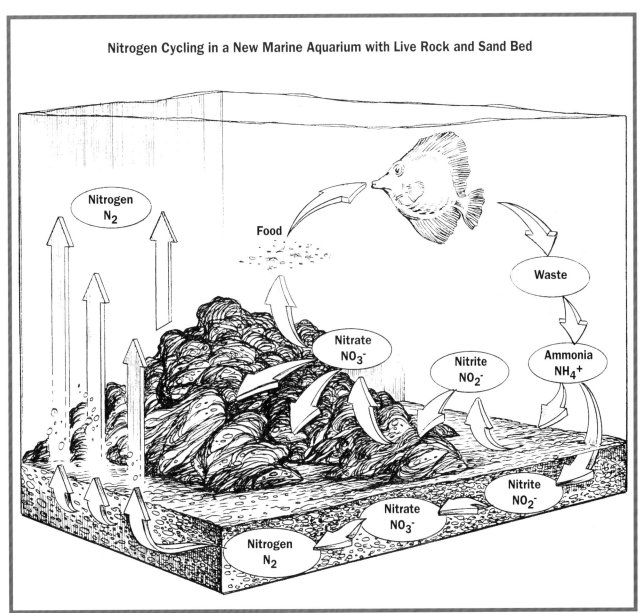

Nitrogen Cycling in a New Marine Aquarium with Live Rock and Sand Bed

A more natural, modern approach to breaking down waste products employs live rock and coral sand for complete biological filtration.

Once this occurs, anything trapped in the filter almost immediately begins to be broken down and is converted into dissolved, undesirable waste compounds that are then flushed back into the aquarium.

Therefore, in order for a mechanical filter to perform its job properly, it needs to be cleaned regularly. Once a week is adequate, although twice a week is better. One of the best ways to provide mechanical filtration for a smaller aquarium is through the use of a canister filter. These external filters draw water in from a screened intake tube in the tank and pass it through a media-filled canister. The canister can utilize various types of mechanical media (usually in concert with chemical media, such as granular activated carbon) to filter the water. After passing through these layers of filtration media, the water is then pumped back into the tank, providing an additional source of circulation. A number of manufacturers make these filters, and for the most part they all function reasonably well.

When selecting one, the main consideration should be the reliability of the pump portion of the filter as well as the ease with which the filter can be shut down, opened for cleaning, then restarted. These housekeeping considerations are crucial, because breaking the filter down for cleaning needs to be quick and simple. Otherwise, it becomes a dreaded chore that doesn't get done and the filter will inevitably become choked with detritus and bacteria. Canister filters with shut-off valves and quick-disconnect fittings on both the intake and outflow lines will allow cleaning without having to break and then restart the siphon and reprime the pump.

Other choices among mechanical filters include hang-on-the-tank power filters, diatomaceous earth filters, and pressurized systems using pleated fiber cartridges.

External power filters that are mounted to the tank are very simple to maintain and highly popular with freshwater hobbyists. Most are underpowered for use in all but very small marine systems, with limited pumping ability and insufficient space for mechanical media. These units do have the advantage of being open and

Custom-built cabinetry for this Jeffrey Turner-designed 220-gallon system neatly encloses all lighting and filtration equipment.

easy to clean (even without stopping the filter), and several heavy-duty models are worthy of consideration on average-sized starter (40-to-50-gallon) marine tanks.

Diatomaceous earth (DE) is a fine white power consisting of the skeletons of microscopic marine diatoms. In special filters, it forms a wetted barrier that very effectively removes even fine suspended particles. DE is so efficient that it can be used to "polish" cloudy water rapidly but is not practical for constant use as it clogs too easily.

Pressure filters employing fiber cartridges, as in some swimming pool systems, do an excellent job of clearing particulates from aquarium water, but many aquarists have found the cartridges need frequent cleaning to prevent dramatic drops in the rate of water flow through the filter. Some aquarists with large fish collections find that cartridge filters are a great help in keeping the water clear of particulates, and others simply like to have a pressure filter available to clarify the tank quickly after cleaning or other disturbance.

While a mechanical filter does help considerably in overall maintenance, many successful tanks employ no active mechanical filtration, except during periodic cleaning sessions when detritus is siphoned out of the tank (and the sump, if one is being used). With live rock, efficient protein skimmers, and adequate circulation from powerheads, mechanical filters can become optional, although the majority of marine systems use them.

CHEMICAL FILTRATION

THIS CATEGORY OF FILTRATION encompasses several very different approaches to removing dissolved wastes from the water: protein skimming, adsorption using activated carbon or ion-exchange resins, and oxidation with the use of ozone (O_3), a technique used by public aquariums and many advanced hobbyists.

In the last decade, much of the increased success in marine keeping can be directly attributed to our understanding of how to remove waste from a closed marine system more efficiently. Chief among the tools that have proved most useful is the protein skimmer or foam fractionator. Protein skimming is not something new. Its use was advocated in the 1960s, but only when the keeping of reef tanks emerged in the late 1980s did the use and availability of protein skimmers increase. Briefly, a skimmer creates a froth of saltwater foam in which a broad range of compounds and particulate matter is attracted to the surface of millions of tiny bubbles that float the wastes out of the system to be collected as a noxious effluent or scum (see page 32).

PROTEIN SKIMMER BENEFITS

IN KEEPING WATER QUALITY HIGH, protein skimming is extremely useful for several reasons. First it helps to remove nitrogenous compounds, particularly proteins, but also phenols, fats, algal spores, and many other substances that bind to proteins, including metals like copper and zinc. By removing waste compounds before they are mineralized, less demand is placed on the tank's bacterial population to break these compounds down, and less nitrate is produced as well.

But a protein skimmer does not distinguish between good and bad compounds to be removed, it simply takes everything it can in the mass of foam that is created. As a result there has been some concern that useful substances such as vitamins and trace elements in the water will become depleted over time when an efficient skimmer is used. To reduce this likelihood, a wide-spectrum trace element supplement can be added weekly, and vitamins should occasionally be added to the fishes' diet.

An additional advantage conferred by the protein skimmer is that having a large volume of water come into contact with air bubbles helps to keep the tank well oxygenated. Furthermore, the active mixing of air and water provides other useful gas-exchange functions, including the removal of carbon dioxide (CO_2) from the system. When allowed to accumulate, CO_2 tends to form carbonic acid, moving the pH of the system lower than its optimum level of 8.1 to 8.4. Even if the protein skimmer isn't always producing a great deal of foam or dark scum, it continues to assist in keeping the general water quality of the tank high.

"IN THE END, HOWEVER, THERE IS NO ONE PRODUCT OR SECRET FOR MAINTAINING HIGH WATER QUALITY IN A SALTWATER AQUARIUM. THE ABSOLUTE ESSENTIALS, ASSUMING THE WATER IS GOOD TO BEGIN WITH, ARE VIGOROUS CIRCULATION AND PROPER TEMPERATURE."

■ ■ ■

GRANULAR ACTIVATED CARBON

WHILE PROTEIN SKIMMING is a cornerstone of the natural, live rock-based saltwater setup (sometimes known as the "Berlin Method," for the place where it was first popularized), it still does not extract every compound that should be removed, especially those that cause yellowing of the water. German aquarists refer to these yellowing agents as *gelbstoff* and routinely keep mesh bags of granular activated carbon in their filtration systems to adsorb complex dissolved waste compounds. Anyone who has kept a freshwater tank is probably familiar with the small black chunks of "charcoal" that were placed above the angel hair or filter floss in the corner box filter. Granular activated carbon (GAC) is basically a more sophisticated and more expensive version of freshwater hobbyist "charcoal."

Activated carbon can be made from a number of substances, including soft coal, coconut shells, bone, or wood. The best products are normally made from bituminous or lignite coal and contain no nitrate or phosphate residue. Activated carbon is made in a two-step process. First the base material is cut or molded to the appropriate size and shape and dehydrated by heating it to over 400 degrees C in the absence of air. In the second step, where the "activation" occurs, the carbon is heated to 800 to 950 degrees C in the presence of steam. Each grain of carbon contains a multitude of microscopic pores. This high heat opens up the pores by burning off any material that clogs them, while the steam washes the burned material away.

These open pores will trap many types of substances, including proteins, copper, ozone, dyes, iodine, heavy metals, drugs, and dissolved organics. GAC is especially useful at removing the compounds that turn a tank yellow over time. Like the protein skimmer, activated carbon is indiscriminate in terms of the compounds it removes. When this material is used, essential trace elements will need to be replenished.

Over time, the pores in the activated carbon become clogged and lose their adsorption abilities. Because these rates of blockage vary depending upon the type of carbon used and the water conditions, numerous methodologies have evolved concerning how carbon should be used and how often it should be replaced. These practices range from using a small amount of carbon and changing it often to using a large amount that is partially removed and replaced at regular intervals.

I think the best advice is to start with a moderate amount of carbon (roughly 4 to 6 tablespoons for each 10 gallons of water in the system) and replace half of it when the water starts to turn yellow. To get the most activity out of the carbon, have the water flow through it after larger particles and detritus have already been removed by mechanical filtration. For this reason, placing the carbon in an external or canister filter, or even a small submersible (in-tank or in-sump) power filter is a good idea.

In addition to activated carbon there are numerous compounds on the market containing ion-exchange resins and other compound-specific eliminators. The claims made about these products are often exaggerated, and the aquarist should always exercise caution. Simple activated carbon in granular form, rather than pellets, is a time-tested filtration aid for a wide variety of water pollutants. It is usually better to use a simple compound with known effects than one with undocumented results.

In the end, however, there is no one product or secret for maintaining high water quality in a saltwater aquarium. The absolute essentials, assuming the water is good to begin with, are vigorous circulation and proper temperature. To combat the accumulation of potentially toxic wastes, the aquarist can use a combination of biological, mechanical, and chemical filtration—with regular small water changes as the key to correcting many problems and imbalances.

CHAPTER 3

LIVE ROCK

Nature's Biological Filter: How to Buy and Tame It

LIVE ROCK, MORE THAN ANY NEW INVENtion or technological wonder, has emerged as the saltwater filtration breakthrough of the century and the aquarist's best ally. In fact, nothing has changed the level of success in keeping marine fishes more than the introduction of live rock as the essential element in modern, well-balanced saltwater aquariums.

While the complete biological workings of live rock remain to be scientifically documented, we know very well what the end effects are on home aquariums: water quality rises, livestock losses drop, and maintenance chores are greatly simplified. With no moving parts, live rock can function as a water purifier for years without adjustment or removal from the tank.

Left: one of the author's live-rock-based systems with a large array of fishes and corals. **Above:** attractive branching Fiji rock.

As an added plus, aquariums decorated with live rock are more attractive and visually interesting—all without the controversial use of dead, bleached coral skeletons. Live rock provides a much more natural-looking environment—an aquascape that appeals both to human observers and reef fishes that use it both as a stress-relieving shelter and a natural foraging ground.

It may help to think of a good piece of live rock as a self-contained biological filter—a sort of stony sponge with a tremendous surface area, much of it hidden internally—that arrives preloaded with rich populations of beneficial microbes. These bacterial cultures proliferate in the presence of dissolved organic pollutants, collectively working to break down toxic fish wastes completely, yielding harmless, odorless nitrogen gas.

Collected from beds of rubble created by past storms, most live rock is nothing more than naturally broken pieces of coral (often fast-growing species of

Acropora and *Porites*) that have been colonized and invaded by many, many forms of life, including bacteria, algae, marine worms, sponges, bryozoans, and corals. It is not uncommon to find crabs, snails, sea urchins, and the larval forms of shrimps and other crustaceans clinging to the rock. Even rather lifeless pieces of rock routinely astonish aquarium keepers when they blossom with pink, purple, and lavender coralline algae, lovely green macroalgae, encrusting corals, bryozoans, tunicates, and myriad other species.

Unlike the bleached coral skeletons used to decorate traditional saltwater tanks, live rock does not involve the harvesting and sacrifice of large, living colonies of hard coral. For the most part, the choice pieces that are hand-picked by collectors and coveted by aquarists are at least several years old, eroded by wave action and tumbling in the rubble, and shaped by the attacks of boring, burrowing, and grazing reef animals. With responsible harvest practices, live rock should be an infinitely renewable source. With care, it can be sustainably collected by hand, without the infamous dynamiting, dredging, and mechanical means often used to gather large volumes of coral for road building and construction projects.

Freshly imported Samoan rock showing a gnarly surface structure. Colorful coralline algae should reappear in time.

BENEFITS OF LIVE ROCK SYSTEMS

1. Greater biological stability.
2. Better survivability of fishes and invertebrates.
3. Lower maintenance.
4. More attractive aquascaping—more natural fish coloration and behaviors.
5. Avoids use of bleached or dyed coral skeletons, whose harvest is opposed by many marine biologists.

CURED VS. FRESH

WHEN BUYING LIVE ROCK there is one major option that must be considered, no matter what type of material is chosen. All live rock is classified as "cured" or "uncured."

Almost all live rock is plucked from the ocean and shipped either moist or virtually dry to the dealer or hobbyist. (The better suppliers pack the rock with damp newspaper in plastic bags within insulated foam boxes that are, in turn, boxed in cardboard. Others simply stack the rock, unprotected, in the cheapest possible shipping boxes.) Live rock is shipped without water to reduce the large freight cost that would occur if it were shipped submerged. Arriving and promptly sold in a dry or moist state, it is "uncured" or "fresh."

As a result of the almost-dry shipping method, many of the organisms present on the rock perish or begin to die, starting a release of ammonia and hydrogen sulfide gas that can last for several weeks after the rock has been immersed in water. Once this die-off has completely ceased and the remaining organisms have stabilized, this rock is considered "cured."

Some distributors and dealers have holding facilities to cure live rock, and the beginning hobbyist will find that this ready-to-use material provides a new tank with an almost instant biological filter with little waiting, smell, or fuss, although generally at a higher cost.

CURE YOUR OWN

THE PREMIUM PRICE charged for cured rock often motivates aquarists to buy freshly imported material and cure their own. I have been using the same curing method for years with good results.

Before bringing any live rock home, you should have an ample supply of saltwater mixed up, aged for several days and adjusted to the usual temperature and specific gravity range of your aquarium (74 to 78 degrees F, 1.022 to 1.026 specific gravity). After removing the live rock from the shipping box, it should be rinsed in a saltwater bath. This is done in order to shake free any detritus that has settled on it as well as to remove any grossly dead organisms, which should be minimal if it has been partially cured in the dealer's tanks.

Upon completion of rinsing, the rock should be inspected and any dead or unwanted organisms (bristleworms, algae, sponges, etc.) removed with forceps, tweezers, or an old toothbrush. Dead organisms are usually readily apparent by their white or black color, limp structure, or offensive smell. If the rock was shipped dry, any sponges that are growing on the rock should be removed. This is important, because sponges that are exposed to air for any length of time usually die as a result of their system not having a means for getting rid of air trapped in their tissues. Also sponges tend to die slowly, so while they may appear alive on the rock, they are often in the process of dying and can release organics into the water for an extended period of time.

The worst offender is the Chicken Liver Sponge (*Chondrilla nucula*), a shiny black or dark brown encrusting species often found on the under surfaces of Atlantic or Caribbean rock. If not removed promptly, it may take several weeks or months to die off completely, releasing organics the entire time. I try to eliminate any fragment of this sponge from incoming live rock, although some reef aquarists have had good luck maintaining it in their systems.

All of the macroalgae should also be plucked from the rock. Most of these algae will have died during the trip, releasing nutrients, so it's best to get them off the rock prior to starting the curing process. (Amazingly, new growths of desirable macroalgae and even healthy sponges will often reappear on live rock weeks or even months after curing, if the conditions are right.)

I prefer to cure all of the live rock at once, as it can be highly detrimental to add any new, uncured rock to an established tank. The ammonia and nitrate levels can skyrocket with each addition, possibly causing the tank's inhabitants to die or starting an unwanted bloom of slime algae. (See page 64 for an alternative to in-tank curing.)

(See page 64 for an alternative to in-tank curing.)

> ### CURING TIP
> To reduce the odor from curing live rock, run a power filter filled with activated carbon, changing the media when it loses its effectiveness.
>
> ■ ■ ■

CURING CONDITIONS

TO CURE ROCK QUICKLY and effectively, two important processes need to be happening. First, vigorous water circulation must be in place. By providing strong water movement, any material that dies will be blown off the rock. In addition, strong water circulation will prevent detritus from settling on the rock and smothering whatever is underneath. To produce this water movement, multiple powerheads are necessary. To remove localized areas of decay, a turkey baster can be used to blow away the white film or patches of black that typically form on curing rock. The second process necessary for proper curing is good protein skimming. During curing, a skimmer will extract voluminous quantities of foul-smelling foam, pulling noxious material out of the water before it further degrades and pollutes the tank. In addition, the skimmer will help to add oxygen to the water so that anaerobic conditions don't develop.

During curing, and as the die-off of organisms progresses, it will be necessary to do some partial water changes. This will not only help rid the tank of some of the wastes and dilute the ammonia concentration, but it will also help reduce the inevitable odor. To facilitate the removal of detritus, the powerheads should first be shut off for 30 minutes and the suspended material allowed to settle. It can then be siphoned off the bottom and the surfaces of the rock, with the siphon tube used to draw any pockets of dead material from all obvious nooks and crevices. The water removed is then replaced with new saltwater that has been allowed to age for at least a couple of days.

During the first week or two, it may be necessary to do this every other day, particularly if there is a significant die-off and a strong smell. (A good protein skimmer and a filter packed with activated carbon will help reduce the amount of odor released.) Once the worst of the die-off has subsided, water changes of about 10 to 20% may be necessary only once or twice a week until the rock is fully cured.

The curing process is complete when there is no

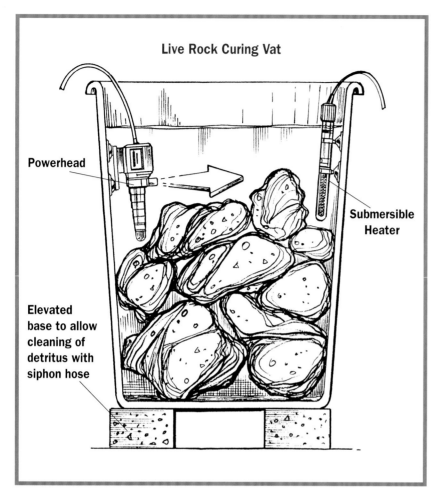

Live Rock Curing Vat

Powerhead

Submersible Heater

Elevated base to allow cleaning of detritus with siphon hose

Many aquarists prefer to cure new live rock in a tank or container outside the main living area of the home, to avoid odor problems. One simple curing system consists of nothing more than a clean saltwater-filled plastic trash can, a powerhead pump, and a heater.

longer any noticeable die-off from the rock and the tank itself has the clean smell of the ocean, free of any hint of decay or hydrogen sulfide. Ammonia and nitrite levels should both measure zero. While the curing process is progressing, livestock, food, or additives should not be added to the tank. Some aquarists prefer to leave the lights off during this period to prevent algal growth. I tend to use the lights, but for a shorter photoperiod than will occur when the tank is fully running. This provides enough light for coralline algae to grow, but not so much that undesirable microalgae will bloom in the presence of a rich broth of nutrients.

The full curing process for fresh rock usually takes 4 to 6 weeks, depending upon where and how the rock was harvested, the amount of time it was exposed to air, the ambient air temperature during shipping, and other

shipping conditions. Obviously, rock that has been partially cured by a distributor or aquarium shop will finish curing more quickly once it has been brought home.

A few important words about the odor of curing live rock: it can be rank. In setting up new tanks, I have had this smell range from mild (the smell of decaying algae) to strong (the aroma of decomposing carcasses). So if your household is not tolerant of strong odors, the alternative to curing the live rock in its aquarium is to cure it in a garage or other remote, heated space. (Outdoors or in a semi-open shelter is ideal, if you have a spot that has electricity, protection from the rain, and mild temperatures.) I have found that an inexpensive 32-gallon Rubbermaid plastic garbage can, equipped with a powerhead and heater, is perfect for curing live rock. (I elevate the vat on blocks, making it simple to siphon detritus off the bottom during curing.)

If this alternative is chosen, the pieces of rock should be physically lifted and moved around every few days. This is important because in an opaque garbage can, it is impossible to see the rock on the bottom and any dead material will tend to accumulate there. It may also be necessary to do a few more partial water changes, particularly if the smell is especially offensive. (Rotating the rock between two garbage cans or other curing vats is a good option. Shake each piece vigorously underwater in a bucket or tub and brush away any dying material before moving it to a container with clean saltwater.)

Coping with this additional handling and the expense of weeks of water changes may not seem worth all the time and bother, especially for setting up a modest-sized first tank. You may simply decide to start by purchasing already-cured live rock. Knowing what is involved, it becomes easier to understand the premium prices cured rock can fetch. However, for anyone setting up a large system or a reef aquarium requiring a large amount of rock, curing it yourself can result in substantial savings. In addition, careful, attentive handling can help preserve many of the organisms that might otherwise be lost in bulk curing systems.

BUYER'S GUIDE TO LIVE ROCK

WHEN IT COMES TO BUYING live rock, there are many choices, grades, types, and price levels. However, the quality of the live rock chosen will have a significant impact on the appearance and long-term success of your aquarium.

Advertisements for live rock often list different types, such as base rock, turf rock, rubble rock, worm rock, or reef rock. Each of these rock types has different characteristics, depending on the depth and water conditions where it has been harvested. The characteristics of the rock also differ from one geographical region to another, as well as from one reef zone to the next. The price is often directly related to the amount of coverage by pink, purple, or lavender coralline algae, and this often depends on the depth from which the rock was collected.

BASE ROCK

BASE ROCK GENERALLY REFERS TO large bulky pieces of live rock that have either been buried under sand or under other pieces of rock. This rock usually does not contain a lot of external life or coralline algae, and it fetches much lower prices than premium grades of live rock. Base rock may be infiltrated with sand or silt, and it needs to be rinsed thoroughly before beginning the curing process.

This rock, as its name implies, is an appropriate foundation for an aquarium reef, with more expensive

---

---

and more decorative rock set upon it for the finished aquascape. Using this rock for the bottom of the mini-reef structure is much better than using dry or dead rock. I strongly urge you to avoid using dry rock to cut corners and save money. Dry or dead rock introduces the risk of bringing toxic contaminants into your tank that are not present in live rock, and lava rock or feather rock, which is of volcanic origin, also seems to act as a magnet for detritus accumulation. As a result, undesirable blooms of microalgae frequently establish themselves on these rocks.

For the beginning aquarist with a limited budget, the entire tank can be stocked with base rock. Look for a store with an inventory of live rock that has been in their tanks for many weeks or even months. Some of this will be premium rock with fine shapes that has been downgraded to the base rock price because it has lost the color and encrusting organisms that reef aquarists desire. It still comes with the appropriate bacterial cultures, however, and will easily serve all the necessary biological filtration functions in a fish-only tank. Under proper lighting and good water conditions, the appearance of base rock can be dramatically restored in some cases.

Typical "base rock" bears very few interesting, visible life forms but is inexpensive and can serve as a mini-reef foundation. Be wary of recycled rock from drug-treated systems.

Pacific turf rock bears a full crop macroalgae, which will typically die back temporarily if not removed, but should later reemerge.

Large pieces of Fiji reef rock like this one make for a stable structure and offer many natural hiding places for smaller fishes.

Be wary, however, of taking base rock that has been returned from another aquarist's system. If the tank was dosed with copper or other drugs, the rock will effectively be dead for some time and may even have absorbed copper into its surfaces. Be sure to ask the history of any "recycled" live rock before buying, whatever the price.

TURF ROCK

TURF ROCK IS THE COMPLETE OPPOSITE of base rock in that, if anything, it contains too much life. This rock is taken from the shallow turf zone where many macroalgae species thrive. For best results, I usually pull off any visible green, red, or brown macroalgae. Turf rock may also bring nice coralline algae growth, as well as large populations of undesirable bristleworms.

When cleaning this rock, care should be taken not to get jabbed by one of these pests when reaching under the rock to pick it up. Some live rock handlers routinely use rubber kitchen gloves for protection. Tweezers are also handy for rapidly removing any worms encountered during the initial cleaning process. Watch the bottom of the curing tank for bristleworms that die soon after arrival and remove them.

WORM ROCK

WORM ROCK DIFFERS from the other two types in that it usually contains a number of hard (calcareous) tubeworms living directly in the rock. These are usually quite decorative. The only problem is that worm rock usually comes from water where there is a higher concentration of suspended matter (i.e., higher nutrients) than found in other reef areas. These naturally occurring worms need to be kept in a nutrient-rich environment in order to remain healthy. If too much worm rock is used in the aquarium, a risk of polluting the water develops because of the amount of suspended food that must be added on a regular basis to keep the tubeworms alive. Conversely, if these animals are not adequately fed, they may die and pollute the tank as they decompose, especially during the curing process.

REEF ROCK

FOR MOST SITUATIONS, reef rock or rubble rock will be the aquarist's best choice. It can be found in irregular rocky shapes, branching forms, and flat plates. This type of rock usually consists of the pieces of old coral skeletons that have broken off and fallen close to the reef in relatively shallow water. As a result reef rock contains the best growth of coralline algae, as well as small colonies of other animal and plant life. Depending on its source, it can contain colonies of live corals as well as tunicates, bryozoans, zooanthids, sponges, and sea squirts.

In reef tanks, this type of rock should make up the bulk of the live rock structure. For the new marine aquarist, this premium reef rock is also desirable but not essential. To economize, a reefscape might be constructed largely of base rock, with one or more pieces of premium reef rock to "top off" the structure.

Aquacultured rock from waters off the Gulf Coast of Florida often carries colorful sponges, which may survive if properly shipped.

Pacific branching rock can be used to dress the top of the reef and create a complex, colorful, and natural-looking aquascape.

AQUACULTURED ROCK

IN RECENT YEARS, a new type of material has entered the market in large quantities: aquacultured live rock. This rock differs from all the others in that it was collected as terrestrial rock, usually coral limestone, that was quarried dry and then placed into the ocean. Aquacultured rock is an attempt to replace and replicate the live rock that the aquarium hobby has been removing for the past 10 years. This rock is similar in consistency to live rock previously taken from the Florida Keys and Gulf of Mexico. Collection of wild rock is now banned in Florida waters, but since most of the available aquacultured rock is now cultivated there, it contains similar organisms to that found on wild Florida rock. This rock is often quite dense and makes a good base. Most aquacultured rock has now been underwater for at least 2 years and is starting to become nicely colonized by reef invertebrates.

ATLANTIC ROCK

NOT ONLY DOES THE ZONE where the rock was cultured create its characteristics, but so does the body of water. Caribbean, Atlantic, or Gulf rock can be very densely structured. Some Atlantic rock is heavy and bricklike, having originated as ultra-dense arms of Elkhorn Coral or calcium carbonate bedrock. This material is acceptable, but not very porous and less than ideal for a marine aquarium. Some newer sources in Central America and Brazil have provided some exceptionally nice rock, but it is not always readily available.

PACIFIC ROCK

LIVE ROCK HARVESTED from the Pacific Ocean is widely available to aquarists and often far less dense than its Atlantic counterparts. This rock is usually more irregular in shape, with a gnarly structure or many branches. It contains more nooks, crannies, and open spaces and typically weighs about half as much as a like volume of Atlantic rock.

Pacific rock is currently being collected from Fiji, Samoa, Tonga, Indonesia, Sri Lanka, and the Marshall Islands. It can be more expensive than its Atlantic counterparts due to the increased costs of shipping. However, less of it (by weight) is required to fill a given space than dense Atlantic rock. The open structure and myriad creatures that often arrive on Pacific reef rock make it the preferred choice of many reef aquarists.

Be aware, however, that two shipments of Pacific rock, even from the same locale, can differ greatly. The level of quality depends on how the rock was handled after harvesting and during shipping. If this rock sits in the boat, on the dock, or on a landing beach for any length of time, dry and in the hot sun, most life on it will perish. During shipping, since there is little water around it for insulation, any remaining life on the rock will be killed if the rock is left to sit in boxes in hot or freezing conditions. Before placing an order for Pacific rock, try to see (and smell) a sample from the same supplier, or get a good recommendation from your dealer or another aquarist.

ROCKSCAPING

EITHER DURING THE CURING PROCESS or right after, live rock should be placed close to its final position in the tank. The positioning of the rock is crucial for several reasons. The animals present on the rock should be placed in a position close to the way they were situated in the wild. That is, if corals and other invertebrates as well as coralline algae were facing upward or sideways to capture strong light or strong water movement, that is how they should be oriented when placed in the tank. It does not make sense to position light-loving organisms upside down—this will only result in further die-offs.

The live rock structure must be stable so that there is no danger it will ever topple over and crack the tank or injure any inhabitants. (Eels are sometimes victims of live rock slides.) The structure also needs to be as open

as possible to provide hiding places for the tank's residents. More importantly, however, this open structure must allow water to move readily around and through it so that detritus does not tend to settle in any one spot.

Resist any tendency you may have to fit the pieces of rock tightly together as if you were trying to build a brick or stone wall.

The final consideration should be to arrange the live rock so that it is aesthetically pleasing and mimics, at least in part, the look of an actual reef. Rather than building a uniform wall or pile, construct one or more peaks and various grooves, channels, or islands (see diagrams below).

It is not necessary to pile the rock all the way to the surface. The usual rule of thumb recommends 2 pounds of dense (Atlantic-type) rock per gallon or 1 pound of lighter (Pacific-type) rock per gallon. Given the greater

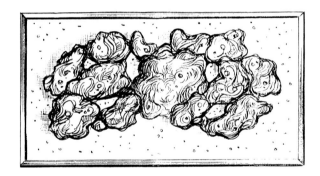

ISLAND FORMATION: this simplest possible aquarium layout, with a loosely assembled central mound, creates a formation that suggests a tropical isle or a patch of coral. Open perimeter space allows ample room for active fishes and glass-cleaning maintenance.

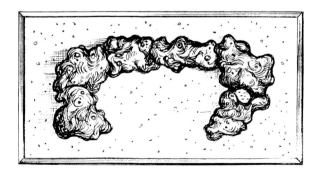

ATOLL FORMATION: this aquascape is a simple variation on the plan above, but with an open sandy area in the center of the rock to give the impression of a protected underwater lagoon. The design is highly adaptable, with height variations adding interest to the view.

variability of live rock available today, these guidelines simply don't work in all cases. Rather than choosing a set number of pounds per gallon, it is much more practical to add rock until roughly one-third to one-half of the tank volume is loosely occupied. This quantity of rock will be more than adequate as a biological filter.

If you like massive rockwork displays, more can be added, but not so much that active fishes are left without enough swimming space. (Many conventional reef tanks have up to two-thirds of their volume stacked with live rock, more to serve as perches for colonies of coral than out of biological necessity.)

Ideally, you may be able to hand-pick cured live rock from your dealer's tanks and thereby take just enough to fill the space you desire. When buying from local stock, you can easily return to buy additional pieces, if needed.

SETUP TIP

Leave enough space between the live rock and the glass for your hand to fit in easily. Test the layout with a cleaning brush to ensure access to the insides of the front and side panels.

■ ■ ■

Ordering uncured live rock presents more of a challenge in determining correct quantities; a dealer or seasoned aquarist can often supply needed advice.

HIDDEN FRAME METHOD

ONE WAY TO REDUCE THE AMOUNT of live rock needed is to place it on top of a framework. This framework can be built out of ½-inch PVC pipe and elbow fittings easily found in a hardware store or plumbing-supply center. The pipe is then fashioned into little cubes and the live rock placed upon these cubes (see illustration). This method not only saves money by allowing for the use of fewer pieces of live rock, but it also produces a structure that is very open. In addition, with a little imagination, authentic-looking caves and overhangs can be constructed that add to the natural look of the tank. With

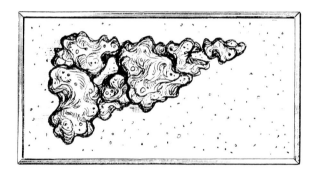

SINGLE PEAK: requiring less rock and leaving more open water than the basic island plan, this aquascape with a high point that slopes down into the sand bed is handsome but simple to build. Essential pieces of aquarium equipment can be hidden behind the rockwork.

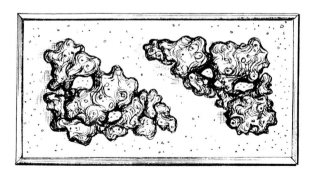

TWO PEAKS WITH CHANNEL: resembling a pair of coral islands with a pass running between them, this layout provides excellent cover for fishes, along with ample swimming space. Rounded or boulderlike pieces of rock can be difficult to use in any of these schemes.

reasonable care in rock placement, the PVC frame can be completely obscured from view.

To make caves and overhangs, several techniques may be used. Live rock can be drilled readily, so one method is to bore holes and place solid PVC rods in the rock to hold it in place. In this way, several small pieces of rock can be joined together to form an arch or an overhang. Using a variation on this technique, a hole large enough to fit a piece of PVC pipe is drilled through the rock and this pipe runs through the entire structure to stabilize an overhang or a cave. Holes should be drilled through the PVC pipe to prevent stagnant areas from developing in the pipe. Similar stability can also be obtained by using black plastic cable ties to anchor pieces of rock to each other. All of these methods may seem rather permanent. They are, for good reason. The more stable the live rock structure, the more likely it is to resist falling over or becoming rearranged. This results in a stable environment, which is more conducive to the inhabitant's long-term well-being.

Another way of adding permanence and stability to the rockscape is by using one of the new saltwater-safe waterproof epoxies that have come on the market recently. The two that I have had the most experience with are Devcon 11600 and Aquarium Systems' Holdfast Epoxy Stick. Both of these compounds are nontoxic marine epoxies that cure underwater. These two-part epoxies come in a log that needs to be kneaded together until it turns white. Once it does, the piece can be used to attach rocks to each other by placing the epoxy between them and squeezing them together. The rocks need to be held together for at least 40 minutes while the epoxy cures. Rubber bands or cable ties can be used to accomplish this. Even though the epoxy will now seem hard to the touch, it is actually only partially cured and still needs 24 hours to cure fully. No pressure should be placed on the joint until that time has elapsed.

Forget trying to emulate an entire reef; no matter how big the tank, it is not likely to come close to the size of even a small reef. However, it is possible to replicate a small portion of the reef or a tiny patch of fringing or lagoon reef, using only live rock, sand, and some imagination. Unlike bleached corals or artificial decorations, live rock is the most realistic aquascaping material you can buy. The initial expense is repaid in several ways: the rock provides a realistic setting, a living biological filter, and an ongoing source of food and shelter for the tank's inhabitants.

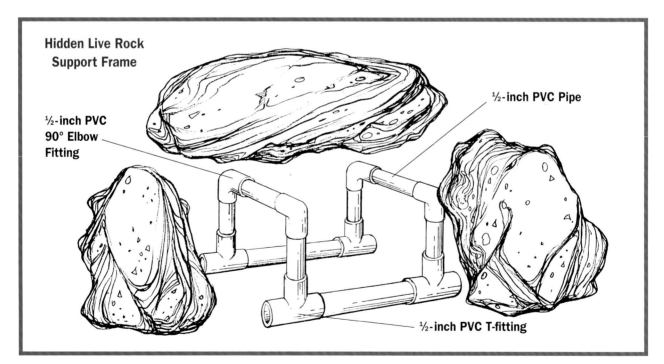

Hidden Live Rock Support Frame

½-inch PVC Pipe

½-inch PVC 90° Elbow Fitting

½-inch PVC T-fitting

A hidden-frame structure, fashioned from half-inch PVC pipe and readily available PVC plumbing fittings, can be made into an infinite variety of supports to elevate rockwork and create the illusion of a massive aquascape but with fewer pieces of live rock required.

LIVING SURPRISES:
THINGS THAT MAY ARRIVE ON LIVE ROCK

Premium Fiji reef rock, nicely encrusted with coralline algae and carrying many unseen organisms.

For months after being placed in an aquarium, live rock can be a source of new, fascinating—and occasionally troublesome—organisms. The following is a list of just a few of the groups that may be encountered:

Amphipods (Order Amphipoda)

Anemones (Phylum Cnidaria)

Barnacles (Class Cirripedia)

Boring clams (Class Bivalvia)

Bristleworms (Phylum Annelida)

Brittle stars (Class Ophiuroidea)

Brown algae (Division Phaeophyta)

Bryozoans or moss animals (Phylum Bryozoa)

Chitons (Class Polyplacophora)

Copepods (Order Copepoda)

Coralline (calcareous red) algae (Division Rhodophyta)

Corals (Phylum Cnidaria)

Crabs (Phylum Arthropoda)

Flatworms (Phylum Platyhelminthes)

Foraminiferans (Phylum Protozoa)

Green macroalgae (Division Chlorophyta)

Hydroids (Order Hydroida)

Limpets (Class Gastropoda)

Mantis shrimps (Order Stomatopoda)

Nudibranchs (Subclass Opisthobranchia)

Oysters (Class Bivalvia)

Peanut worms (Phylum Sipuncula)

Sea hares (Subclass Opisthobranchia)

Sea stars (Class Asteroidea)

Sea urchins (Class Echinoidea)

Snails (Class Gastropoda)

Snapping or pistol shrimps (*Alpheus* spp.)

Sponges (Phylum Porifera)

Terebellid Worms (Class Polychaeta)

Tubeworms (Families Serpulidae and Sabellidae)

Tunicates or sea squirts (Class Ascidiacea)

Zoanthids (Phylum Cnidaria)

CHAPTER 4

ESTABLISHING
A NEW AQUARIUM

From Empty Tank to Living Ecosystem:
A Step-by-Step Guide

ONE OF THE MYTHS of marine aquarium setup describes a day of extreme excitement and pressure, with bags of live fish waiting as the new aquarist frantically hurries to fill and plumb his or her tank. At the end of the day, the tank is glowing and the fishes are happily swimming about their new home. Forget this fairy tale. It is just not the way it happens.

The actual setup can start when all of your equipment and supplies are at hand. At this point, no live or-

Left: reef tank with cave. **Above:** Onespot Rabbitfish (*Siganus unimaculatus*).

> "TAKE YOUR TIME, ADHERE TO THE UNCOMPLICATED PROCEDURE ILLUSTRATED IN THIS CHAPTER, AND LAY A PROPER FOUNDATION FOR THE ANTICIPATED DAY WHEN YOU DO RELEASE YOUR FIRST MARINE FISHES INTO THE CAPTIVE WORLD YOU HAVE CREATED."
>
> ■ ■ ■

ganisms will have been acquired, and the process can move at whatever pace you choose to set. There is no real need for haste, and there should be no expectation that the tank can be filled, stocked, and—voilà!—finished for viewing in a few hours.

Impatience is natural in the early stages, but any aquarium veteran will tell you that haste and skipping fundamental setup steps will almost certainly be followed by regrets. Take your time, adhere to the uncomplicated procedure illustrated in this chapter, and lay a proper foundation for the anticipated day when you do release your first marine fishes into the captive world you have created.

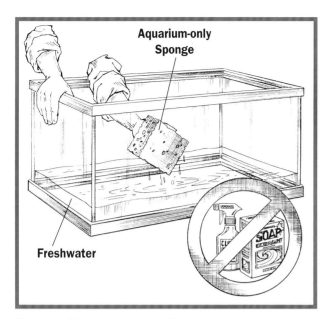

STEP 1: Wash the aquarium with a new sponge and clean water, avoiding the use of any glass cleaners or detergents.

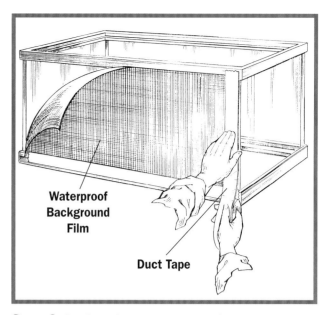

STEP 2: Dry the tank and apply a sheet of colored aquarium background material or two coats of latex paint to the back panel.

STEP 1

CLEAN THE TANK

FOR A NEW AQUARIUM, a preparatory washdown with warm water will remove any dust or film residues from manufacturing, shipping, and storage. Beginning with this cleaning, make it a habit to avoid the use of any soaps, detergents, or glass cleaners in the aquarium or on any equipment that will come in contact with system water. Similarly, any sponges, cleaning rags, or buckets you use must not be contaminated with household, garden, or automotive chemicals—these can be deadly. Designating some containers and tools for "Aquarium Use Only" is a very good idea.

To remove stains, fingerprints, or adhesives from the glass or acrylic surfaces, use white vinegar (acetic acid) and rinse thoroughly with clean water. Never use abrasive scrubbers on acrylic. Be sure to handle the tank with care. Glass aquariums, especially, can easily be cracked or broken when empty if thumped with a tool or dropped even a few inches. (Always have dry hands when carrying or moving an aquarium.)

If the tank has been previously used, it may be wise to disinfect it thoroughly with hydrogen peroxide or a solution of chlorine bleach. Again, white vinegar is a cheap and useful cleaning agent and will help to remove stubborn calcium deposits on used equipment. Be sure to rinse with freshwater after using any peroxide, bleach, or vinegar.

STEP 2

APPLY THE BACKGROUND

FOR THE TYPICAL HOME AQUARIUM, the back or one end of the tank will usually be placed against a wall or away from the viewer. Covering the exterior of this back panel with a sheet of background material or paint will yield a much neater appearance and more realistic aquascaping. It is much simpler to apply the background while access is unrestricted and the tank is not yet in position. (Having to place a background on a full tank with various pieces of equipment, hoses, and cords already in place is a nuisance.)

If using a waterproof sheet of background material, cut it to size and tape all four edges with heavy duty waterproof tape, such as duct tape. Painting the background glass

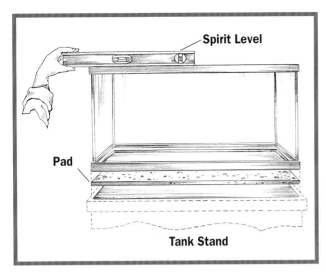

STEP 3: Using a carpenter's spirit level, level the stand, place a pad under the tank, then be sure that the tank itself is level.

is more permanent; two coats of any quick-drying latex paint will do. (Acrylic tanks are tricky to paint but can be ordered with black or blue back panels.)

STEP 3

LEVEL STAND & TANK

FIRST, BE SURE that the aquarium stand (or whatever surface will support the tank) is level and that it will easily handle the weight of the tank when full. Use a carpenter's spirit level to ensure that the tank is level front to back and side to side. If a level is not available, at least give the stand a rough check using a water glass. Fill the glass half full, place it on a known level surface, such as a kitchen counter, and mark a thin, straight horizontal line on the outside of the glass. Place the glass on the stand and note if the water level deviates from the marked line. If the stand is not level, adjust or shim the base as needed.

Before the tank is placed on the stand, a thin layer of Styrofoam or dense furniture-cushioning felt should be placed between the tank and the stand. The Styrofoam or hard felt acts like a shock absorber so that any downward stressors on the tank do not cause the tank to crack. The pad also helps to level the tank and to prevent any pressure cracks from occurring should any gravel or other type of object get trapped between the glass and the stand.

Now, with the tank on the stand and before any water is added, check to ensure that it is level front to back

and side to side. If not, adjust the stand again, as needed. These leveling precautions are necessary to reduce any uneven stresses on the sides of the tank, once filled. A few minutes spent on this task will greatly reduce the likelihood of any leaks occurring over time.

STEP 4

FILL & TEST: WET RUN

NEXT, ALL OF THE EQUIPMENT, but none of the live rock or sand, should be placed in the dry tank. Specifically: without plugging in or turning anything on, the skimmer should be hung on the back, the external filter setup (if one is to be used), and all plumbing connected. Place the powerhead(s) and heater(s) in the back corners where they will be reasonably hidden. Try to envision the flow of water from each of the powered elements and space them accordingly. Be sure all electrical connections are dry and positioned out of the potential path of any splashing or dripping water (see page 39).

At this point fresh, untreated tap water (no salt added) can be used to fill the tank, skimmer, and external filter. (If a countercurrent protein skimmer is being used, the air pump should be turned on prior to the wa-

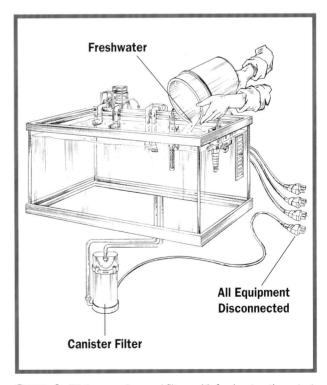

STEP 4: Fill the aquarium and filters with freshwater, then start up and run the system for 24 to 48 hours to test all equipment.

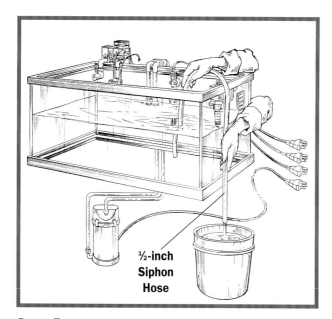 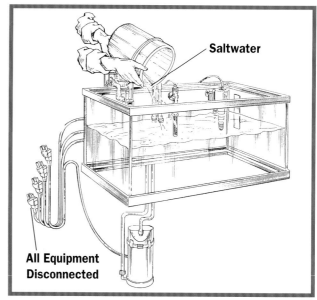

½-inch
Siphon
Hose

Saltwater

All Equipment
Disconnected

STEP 5: Once the tank has been tested for leaks and all equipment checked, the freshwater should be drained, using a siphon hose, and discarded. Refill the aquarium with premixed saltwater or freshwater to which a synthetic marine aquarium salt mix will be added.

ter being added. This is done because it is much easier for the pump to force air through a dry airstone than one soaked with water. Starting with a dry airstone places less initial stress on the air pump.)

You may wish to think of this first filling of water as a "wet run." This water is used to test for leaks in the tank and plumbing as well as to help wash out any dust or manufacturing residues present in the equipment. This filling will help to establish how high the water level should be and how well the water flows through the skimmer and powerheads. (It is a very good idea to draw a line with an indelible marker at the desired water level somewhere on a back corner of the tank. This will be your permanent reference point for keeping the water level topped up and at its proper specific gravity.)

To be sure that nothing is leaking, carefully wipe up all wet spots or stray drops of water on or around the aquarium and all of its water-filled equipment. Let everything run with freshwater for 24 to 48 hours. Check all seams of the tank and all pieces of equipment for leaks. Adjust the heater to the desired level (74 to 78 degrees F) and begin checking the temperature. It should stabilize and not exceed the upper limit (or 80 degrees) after the aquarium lights have been on for 10 to 12 hours.

Chances are excellent that everything will be working fine, but if there are any problems, they should be fixed or adjusted at this time. If you happen to find yourself with a leaking tank or nonfunctional piece of equipment, it should be returned immediately for replacement. (Be sure to keep all guarantees, instruction booklets, and receipts to make returns as painless as possible. Retain the original packaging until all the new gear has proved to be free of defects. If you must bring something back, it is prudent to call ahead. Some problems can be fixed immediately over the telephone. If this isn't possible, you will want to be sure that someone able to give replacements or refunds will be at the store when you bring back the problematic item.)

STEP 5 — DRAIN & REFILL

THE INITIAL FILLING of freshwater can now be drained and the tank filled with premixed saltwater from a mixing vat or reservoir. If you plan to mix the initial batch of saltwater in the tank itself, first fill it with clean freshwater. This new water should be as pure as possible, and it should come out of the cold water tap only. (Hot water tanks are notorious sources of heavy metal contaminants.) If using treated municipal water, add a good tap water treatment or conditioner to neutralize chlorine, chloramine, and heavy metals (see Source Water, page 46).

If using an alternate source of freshwater (purified

water from an aquarium shop, spring water, or water from your own water-treatment equipment), use it now to fill the aquarium, skimmer, and any other external filters.

With the freshwater added, all equipment can be restarted. Let things run until the temperature is brought to your target point and then add the synthetic sea salt. (Salt dissolves more slowly in cold water, and you must take specific gravity readings at the right operating temperature, so it is generally inadvisable to add the salt mix before the water warms up.) Less salt should be added at first, as many tanks have slightly smaller volumes than advertised. Once the salt has been allowed to dissolve for 24 hours, specific gravity readings can be taken and additional salt or freshwater added to reach the desired salinity of 1.022 to 1.026.

The tank should then be allowed to run for a few days as a further check for leakage or equipment problems as well as to allow the newly prepared saltwater to age.

Be sure to check the temperature several times a day during this period, especially while the lights are on. Adjust the heater thermostat(s), if necessary.

STEP 6

ADD LIVE ROCK

ONCE THE PROPER SALINITY and temperature have been established, it is time to add the live rock and possibly the substrate. Adding live rock to a tank with just-mixed saltwater or water of the wrong temperature or salinity can easily kill desirable bacteria and other organisms on the rock. Live rock will survive and recover from many insults, but the better you treat it, the sooner it will cure and the more life it will display. If PVC skeletons are going to be used beneath the rock structure (see page 69), they should be put in place prior to the rock. How and whether substrate is added at this time is determined by the quality and condition of the live rock. If it is cured and well rinsed (in saltwater), it can be arranged in the tank and the substrate added immediately. If the live rock is uncured and you plan to to cure it in the tank, add it now, but be sure to leave the tank bottom bare.

During curing, a substantial amount of detritus will come off the rock and is much more easily siphoned out when the tank bottom is uncovered. After adding the rock, remove any saltwater that rises above the fill line, reserving it for future water changes.

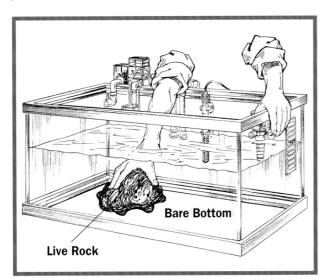

Bare Bottom

Live Rock

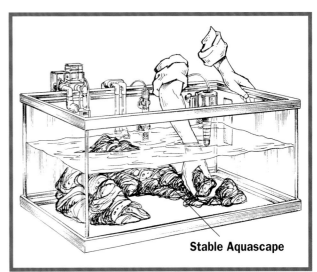

Stable Aquascape

STEP 6: Once the saltwater has cleared and the temperature and pH have stabilized, live rock can be added. Place the larger pieces first, locating them directly on the bottom (with no substrate) and aquascape as desired, leaving ample clearance for future cleaning.

START
QUARANTINE TANK

AT THIS SAME TIME the quarantine tank can be established (see page 113).

CYCLE THE
TANK

CYCLING is an old aquarium term that essentially means allowing nature to take its course. During cycling, bacterial cultures develop and spread within the system, fed by a source of nitrogenous waste (ammonia). Hardy damselfishes and their feed are the classic source of ammonia for a new tank, but live rock works much better. Cycling starts when ammonia can be detected in the water, then progresses through a stage when ammonia declines and nitrite builds. As soon as both ammonia and nitrite (which are toxic, although nitrite is much less of a problem than ammonia) drop to undetectable levels, the tank is pronounced "cycled" and ready for fishes.

SETUP TIPS

■ When placing rocks in a tank, build a sturdy but open structure to allow swimming room for fishes and access for detritus removal during siphoning sessions.

■ Tight heaps of rock or brickwork-like walls are visually uninteresting. If in doubt about an aquascape, follow a simple layout plan (pages 68 to 69), or review photographs of actual reefs for inspiration.

■ ■ ■

Cycling can take anywhere from 1 to 8 weeks, depending on the initial condition of the live rock. With fully cured live rock, only minimal levels of ammonia and nitrite will appear (sometimes none at all) and the system will be ready to receive its first live fishes in short order.

When uncured or partially cured rock is used, the cycling process will often take 3 to 4 weeks—or even up to 8 weeks. During the curing of live rock, the protein skimmer will be pulling out large quantities of material and may need to be emptied of waste daily. Evidence that the curing period is nearing completion is that the quantity of material being removed from the protein skimmer has been greatly reduced. Once the live rock is cured and no additional die-off is seen (or smelled), the ammonia and nitrite levels in the tank should drop to zero. Nitrate concentration, however, can be high at this point, and a 25 to 50% water change with 3-to-4-day-old prepared saltwater should be done to remove as much nutrient-laden water as possible.

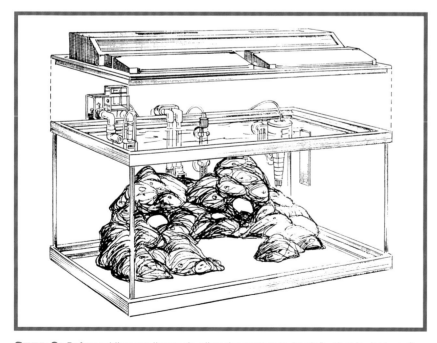

STEP 8: Before adding any livestock, allow the system to "cycle"—that is, let beneficial bacteria develop until water tests show readings of zero ammonia and zero nitrite.

COMPLETE
AQUASCAPE

AT THIS TIME, the live rock should be moved into its final position, if not already situated to your satisfaction. As noted above, the rock should be placed in as open a pattern as possible, with natural-looking peaks, valleys, openings, caves, and overhangs. Try to avoid making a monotonous heap of tightly fitted pieces; fishes and water currents should be able to pass through your rockscape. It usually helps to place the biggest pieces down first, to create a solid foundation. This is where irregularly shaped

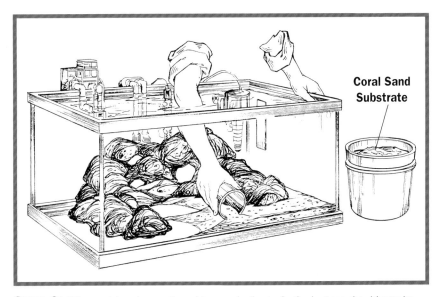

STEP 9: If live rock has been allowed to cure in the tank, the bottom should now be siphoned clean of detritus; once nitrogen cycling is complete, add the coral substrate.

rock is very easy to arrange, while rounded pieces often defy fitting firmly into place. Whatever structure is created, it must be completely stable, with no precariously placed pieces or wobbly sections. Anything loose is certain to slip or fall later (see Rockscaping, page 68).

Once the rockscaping is done, an appropriate substrate can be laid in (see pages 82 to 85). As noted earlier, one of the advantages of using PVC skeletons to support the live rock is that these skeletons will greatly reduce the formation of any dead (anaerobic) spots in the substrate since most of the rock will sit above it. The substrate should be placed all around the bottom of the tank to a depth of ½ to 1 inch. If certain areas cannot be reached, this should not be a concern—the fish and the current will eventually distribute the substrate evenly.

If during the addition of substrate some falls onto the rock, it should simply be blown off using a turkey baster. The substrate should slope down to-

ward the front where detritus can be removed easily.

After the substrate has been added, the tank will appear cloudy, no matter how thorough a job of cleaning was done. This is due to the fine dust that comes from virtually all substrate materials. Suspended sediment from coral sand is harmless at this point and is only a concern in that it will make further aquascaping difficult. Within 24 hours, the tank will have cleared and then the aquascape can be adjusted as necessary for stability and aesthetics.

Once the live rock and substrate are in position, it is usually a good idea not to introduce any livestock or additives for at least a week to let tank conditions stabilize. The only thing that should be added is freshwater to make up for evaporation (check the mark on your tank made in Step 4).

One last trick for the impatient: if you absolutely must have something to watch in the new aquarium as

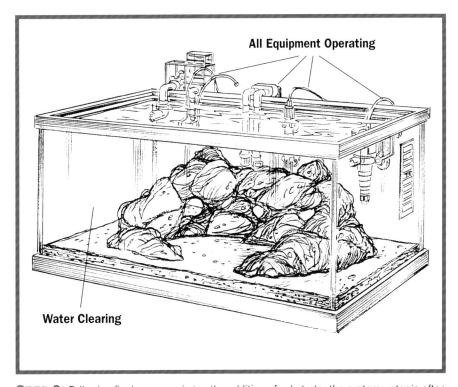

STEP 9: Following final aquascaping or the addition of substrate, the system water is often cloudy, a condition that is normal at this stage; it should clear up within a day.

STEP-BY-STEP CHECKLIST FOR SETTING UP A SALTWATER FISH-ONLY TANK

PLAN THE SYSTEM
Visit local aquarium shops
- ❏ Survey fishes, tanks, stands
- ❏ Learn about the compatibility of desired fishes
- ❏ Ask about marine starter-kit packages and options

Consider the options and design your aquarium
- ❏ Decide on size and location of tank
- ❏ Make a list of equipment needed/wanted
- ❏ Sketch some ideas for tank layout
- ❏ Budget for equipment and livestock
- ❏ Create a simple written system plan
- ❏ Settle on the types of fishes to be kept

PURCHASE EQUIPMENT & SUPPLIES
- ❏ Purchase equipment
- ❏ Order or reserve live rock

SET UP & TEST EQUIPMENT
Prepare aquarium
- ❏ Clean tank
- ❏ Apply tank background
- ❏ Locate and level stand, leaving clearance for electrical connections
- ❏ Set tank in place on underpad
- ❏ Level tank
- ❏ Install all equipment in tank (unplugged)
- ❏ Fill tank and filtration equipment with tap water

Perform wet test
- ❏ Start all equipment
- ❏ Allow tank to run for 24 to 48 hours
- ❏ Check for leaks
- ❏ Check temperature with and without lights on; adjust heater(s)
- ❏ Check protein skimmer for bubble production (no waste will be produced by skimmer until salt and live matter are added to tank)

MIX SALTWATER
- ❏ Mix saltwater in a separate vat, old aquarium, clean plastic garbage can, or other inert container
- ❏ Allow salt to dissolve for 24 hours with a heater and small air or water pump for circulation; adjust specific gravity as necessary

START UP SYSTEM
Empty tank
- ❏ Mark a "fill-to" line on an outside back corner of the tank with an indelible marker representing the permanent water level you wish to maintain with equipment running
- ❏ Shut down all equipment
- ❏ Siphon freshwater out of tank

Refill with saltwater
- ❏ Fill tank and filters with premixed saltwater (if mixing vat is too small to match the initial fill-up requirements of the tank, mix saltwater in the tank)
- ❏ Restart all equipment; adjust water level, if necessary
- ❏ Allow tank to run with equipment on for a few days (protein skimmer will be pulling little or nothing from tank, but is serving a useful function in oxygenation and gas exchange)

Check water parameters
- ❏ Temperature target: 74 to 78°F (23 to 26°C)
- ❏ Specific gravity target: 1.022 to 1.026
- ❏ pH target: 8.1 to 8.3
- ❏ Add freshwater as needed to fill line to make up for evaporation and maintain constant specific gravity

SET UP QUARANTINE TANK
- ❏ At any time during the planning process—but at least 2 weeks prior to buying any fishes—set up a small quarantine tank (see pages 113 to 115)

PREPARE LIVE ROCK
If starting with uncured live rock:
- ❏ Unpack rock and rinse in saltwater
- ❏ Brush and pick away any dead or dying material, including all sponges and plants
- ❏ Place into curing vat or the display aquarium, leaving the bottom of the tank bare (see Aquascape the Tank, below)
- ❏ Follow curing procedures (see page 62)
- ❏ If curing rock in the display aquarium, prepare enough saltwater in an outside container for a 25 to 50% water change

❏ Once rock has cured or most of the die-off has subsided, do aquascaping (see below)

If starting with fully cured and cleaned live rock:

❏ Keep rock wet or damp and at room temperature (70 to 80°F) until placed in the aquarium

❏ Follow steps for aquascaping (see below)

AQUASCAPE THE TANK

❏ Turn off all pumps

❏ Remove heaters to prevent breakage

❏ Lower water level, to allow addition of rock without spillage (reserve saltwater for future water change)

❏ Place live rock in tank, creating the aquascape you desire; use PVC frame, if preferred (see page 69)

❏ Check for loose rock or unstable construction that could lead to a broken or scratched aquarium or livestock injury; stabilize rockscape

ALLOW THE TANK TO CYCLE

❏ With only saltwater and live rock in tank, allow system to run for 3 to 8 weeks, while testing for ammonia, nitrite, nitrate

Test for ammonia

❏ Begin ammonia tests 1 to 3 days after adding live rock and continue testing every 4 days until ammonia levels begin to fall

❏ If starting with cured live rock, ammonia levels may peak by day 3 or may never register

❏ Continue ammonia tests until level reads zero (approximately day 20)

Test for nitrite

❏ Begin nitrite testing when ammonia level drops, approximately day 8, and continue testing at least every 4 days

❏ If ammonia never appears, nitrite may also not become detectable

❏ Continue nitrite tests until level reads zero (approximately day 21)

Test for nitrate

❏ Begin nitrate tests after ammonia and nitrite levels become undetectable (about day 21); the presence of nitrite will give a false high nitrate reading

❏ Testing should show a leveling off of nitrate at approximately day 45

❏ Begin testing nitrate once a month

❏ By keeping nitrate levels below 10 ppm, the growth of problem algae can be kept to a minimum; if nitrate exceeds 20 ppm, take corrective action (see below)

PERFORM WATER CHANGES

❏ If live rock has been cured in the aquarium and nitrates are high, perform a large (up to 50%) water change, using properly mixed and aged saltwater

❏ Repeat water changes, if needed, until nitrate measures less than 10 ppm

ADD SUBSTRATE

❏ Roughly ¼ to ½ pound of coral sand substrate per gallon of tank volume should be sufficient; substrate layer should be ½ to 1 inch deep

❏ If desired, add a quantity of live sand or sand from a healthy, well-established marine aquarium to introduce beneficial bacteria and microfauna

PURCHASE FIRST FISHES

❏ Determine that quarantine tank is running properly

❏ Purchase two or three fishes that fit into your species plan, along with their appropriate foods

❏ Place fishes in quarantine tank for 3 weeks

❏ Treat fishes in quarantine tank, as necessary

❏ If medicating fishes in quarantine tank, continue to test ammonia levels daily

❏ End of quarantine period should coincide with or come after the end of the rock-curing process

❏ After quarantine is over and fishes are eating well, transfer them to main tank

❏ Test display tank for ammonia daily; level should be zero; if level rises above 0.2 to 0.4, do partial water changes and reduce feeding until level is zero

ADD MORE FISHES

❏ If ammonia level does not rise, more fishes (compatible with existing ones) can be added after proper quarantine period

KEEP THE SYSTEM HEALTHY

❏ Begin regular maintenance (see pages 123 to 131)

❏ Keep log of water tests, livestock additions, losses

❏ Do not overstock or overfeed tank

❏ Keep quarantine tank operating

LIVE SAND: REEF-HARVESTED OR GROW YOUR OWN

Perhaps the premium substrate for any saltwater aquarium is "live sand" collected from coral reef areas and shipped wet to preserve its large populations of bacteria and beneficial benthic (bottom-dwelling) invertebrates. Composed of broken down fragments of corals, shells, and other calcareous skeletons, live sand is currently being collected off Florida, in the Gulf of Mexico, and in the Fiji Islands.

Good-quality live sand contains bacteria, amphipods, copepods, burrowing mollusks, and many other crawling and burrowing invertebrates, especially worms. There is currently a growing interest in promoting the presence of these forms of life in reef aquariums, both to assist in the breakdown of wastes and to produce an ongoing supply of small live food items for captive fishes.

There have been many reports of live sand beds helping to reduce nitrate levels. This approach usually calls for an artificial platform to raise a deep (approx. 4-inch) bed of sand off the bottom, creating a plenum with a stagnant (approx. 1-inch deep) pool of water underneath the substrate (much like an undergravel filter plate, but with no active water circulation through the space under the gravel).

This is generally called the Jaubert System, after the method demonstrated by Dr. Jean Jaubert at the Monaco Aquarium. The system seems to work best with light bioloads, and not all hobbyists have had uniform success with this approach. Some aquarists have shown that live sand can be utilized directly on the bottom of the tank, without the plenum, and still have greatly reduced (or zero) nitrate levels. (Even a ½-inch layer of live sand has been shown to have some utility in lowering nitrate levels.)

One problem is obtaining truly "live" sand. In too many cases, the sand has been subjected to killing heat, cold, or long shipping and storage. Some aquarists now prefer to start with a large quantity of new (dry) coral sand and inoculate it with a small quantity (a pound or two) of very high quality live sand—or sand from a healthy, established reef tank.

As with other substrates, live sand should only be introduced after the live rock has been placed in the aquarium and fully cured. (The ammonia overload from curing rock can kill delicate sand organisms.) The sand should then be added so that it covers the tank bottom around the live rock and is about ¾ inch deep. The rock should not rest on the sand, as this can allow dead (anaerobic) areas to form and generate poisonous hydrogen sulfide gas.

Successful proponents of live sand recommend that living sand sifters be added to the tank. These animals help to remove detritus that has settled in the sand and, by constantly stirring it up, keep the sand from compacting. This reduces the likelihood that dead spots will form. The marine creatures that can perform this important function include gobies, hermit crabs, and brittle stars, to name a few. (Where no sand sifters are present, the owner can occasionally stir the sand bed lightly with a plastic rod to loosen any clumping that has occurred.)

Live sand can also assist in buffering the tank's water while providing a hiding place for fishes that need to burrow. When considering substrate alternatives, live sand should be viewed as a good option if a source of high-quality material is available.

For most new aquarists, however, a good dry substrate of coral origin—coral sand, reef sand, crushed coral, or aragonite—will suffice. In time, it will accumulate a population of some of the same organisms as those found in live sand, especially if good-quality live rock is present.

rock cures (this itself can be fascinating, if you observe closely) and before the water conditions settle down and your first fishes go through quarantine, buy a small air pump, a length of silicon hose, and a burping clam or other animated water toy.

Seriously, adding new fishes before the tank has stabilized can easily trigger outbreaks of disease that will be difficult to remedy and that may create an ongoing source of problems. (At this point, your quarantine tank should be up and running and you will be able to watch your first fishes there.)

ABOUT SUBSTRATE

THE SUBSTRATE used in a marine system was once of critical importance when the method of filtration was an undergravel plate. Too fine and it worked its way under the filter plate; too coarse and it failed to screen debris properly. While the substrate chosen in a live rock system will still play a role in the long-term success of the tank, it is no longer the key determining factor.

Even though live rock is being used, the substrate still provides a locus on which bacteria can colonize. Just as the live rock maintains colonies of nitrifying bacteria to convert toxic ammonia into less toxic nitrate, so too does the substrate. The greater the bacterial population in a tank, the greater the likelihood that it will overcome problems that occur, such as the sudden death of a fish, overfeeding, or overstocking. Depending on how much of the aquarium floor is covered with exposed sand, the substrate can provide a significant surface area for bacterial colonization.

Another substrate attribute is that it can help buffer the water. The breakdown of proteinaceous materials in a marine aquarium generally results in the pH of the tank becoming more acidic over time, but the type of substrate chosen can help moderate or buffer this lowering of the pH. For this reason, the substrate used should have a large portion of calcium carbonate (an alkaline compound) as part of its composition. The simplest choice is sand of coral origins, usually sold as reef sand, crushed coral, or aragonite. These are all forms of calcium carbonate and will all serve as good aquarium buffers: as organic acids are produced, they will dissolve the substrate very slowly (over a period of years), which will continually moderate the tank's pH.

Sandbox or play sand has no place in a marine aquarium. It is composed of silica, which will feed unsightly brown diatom-film growth and will tend to compact and form anaerobic areas, leading to the production of toxic hydrogen sulfide gas. The right substrate will help keep the tank stable, increasing the likelihood of the inhabitant's long-term survival.

In addition to providing a locus for bacterial colonization and buffering for the tank, substrate performs several other functions. First, it is aesthetically more

---

SETUP TIP

Always add substrate (coral sand) after the live rock structure has been built directly on the floor of the tank. Burrowing livestock can topple rockwork placed atop a bed of sand.

■ ■ ■

TEN COMMON SETUP MISTAKES

1. Impatience: filling the aquarium with saltwater and starting the equipment before: leveling the tank; checking for leaks; testing all equipment and connections.

2. Using synthetic saltwater too soon after it is mixed.

3. Placing live rock too close to aquarium walls, making cleaning difficult or impossible.

4. Stacking live rock like a stone wall rather than in a natural, open structure.

5. Not allowing live rock to cure before introducing any fishes to the aquarium.

6. Not allowing time for the tank to "cycle" and for the populations of beneficial bacteria to become established.

7. Failing to quarantine new fishes.

8. Adding too many fishes too soon.

9. Not adding herbivores (maintenance animals) as soon as green film algae begins to appear.

10. Adding uncured live rock after the system has been stocked with fishes.

THE BAREBONES DESKTOP TANK, OR
A YOUNG AQUARIST'S STARTER SYSTEM

BASICS

❏ 15- or 20-gallon glass aquarium

❏ Fitted light and cover glass or hood

❏ External power filter (100 to 300 gallons/hour) with mechanical filter media (fiber or sponge to catch detritus) and compartment for activated carbon

❏ Small powerhead (100 to 200 gallons/hour)

❏ Cured live rock (10 to 15 pounds)

❏ Coral sand (5 to 10 pounds)

❏ 50-watt heater

❏ Thermometer

❏ Marine salt mix

❏ Net

❏ Cleaning pad

❏ Siphon tube or gravel-cleaning kit

Basic 20-gallon marine desktop aquarium, which requires light stocking and more diligent maintenance procedures than systems with larger volumes.

FISH OPTIONS (3 to 5 total)

❏ 1 to 2 Ocellaris or Percula Clownfish (*Amphiprion ocellaris*; *A. percula*)

OR 1 Cherub Angelfish (*Centropyge argi*)

OR 1 jawfish (Family Opistognathidae)

OR 1 Yellowtail Blue Damselfish (*Chrysiptera parasema*)

PLUS

❏ 1 Royal Gramma (*Gramma loreto*)

OR 1 Orchid, Springer's, or Sankey's Dottyback (*Pseudochromis fridmani; P. springeri; P. sankeyi*)

OR 1 to 2 Golden or Canary Wrasses (*Halichoeres chrysus*)

INVERTEBRATE OPTIONS

❏ 1 to 2 Common Cleaner Shrimp (*Lysmata amboinensis*)

OR 1 Banded Coral Shrimp (*Stenopus hispidus*)

OR 3 to 5 Peppermint Shrimp (*Lysmata wurdemanni*)

PLUS (all optional)

❏ 1 brittle star (Class Ophiuroidea)

❏ 1 small hermit crab (Section Anomura)

❏ 1 to 5 feather duster worms (Families Serpulidae & Sabellidae)

❏ 3 to 5 star shell snails (*Lithopoma* [*Astraea*] spp.)

ENHANCEMENTS/UPGRADES

❏ 2-bulb striplight

❏ Hang-on-tank skimmer

❏ Light timer

WARNING: This aquarium setup will only succeed with the following precautions and regular care:

❏ Do not add additional fishes.

❏ Do not overfeed.

❏ Do not add photosynthetic invertebrates such as corals or anemones.

❏ Replace evaporated water with aged, dechlorinated freshwater at least every other day.

❏ Replace 5 to 10% of the total volume of water with new, aged saltwater each week.

❏ Check and adjust specific gravity, temperature, and condition of filter media weekly.

❏ Replace activated carbon monthly.

❏ Follow normal maintenance procedures (page 123 to 131).

pleasing to look at a tank with substrate. While there are still some tanks being kept with bare bottoms, to most of us these look more like experiments than home aquariums. In addition to the substrate making the tank appear more natural, substrate also increases the well-being of the animals. Some fishes, such as wrasses, jawfishes, and gobies, require substrate for their natural habits: wrasses bury themselves in the substrate to sleep or when threatened; jawfishes and some gobies dig their homes there.

A few other characteristics need to be considered when choosing a substrate. It should not be too coarse or it will trap detritus. It should also not be too small or it will tend to pack down and become anaerobic, allowing pockets of toxic hydrogen sulfide gas to develop. It should be of relatively uniform size or "channeling" will occur, in which the small pieces get packed in between the large pieces, creating anaerobic areas. A roughly spherical substrate will reduce channeling and maximize the exposed surface area. This rounded shape, typical of reef sand or crushed coral, will also decrease the likelihood of having rough edges that can scratch or scrape fishes that come in frequent contact with bottom materials.

In my experience, the best substrate particle is approximately ⅛ inch (2 mm) in diameter, giving maximum surface area with minimal compacting and little detritus accumulation. One substrate that meets all of these criteria is coral sand (aragonite). The next best choices are substrates derived from crushed oyster shells or limestone. These calcium carbonate substrates of marine origin are far superior to dolomite (calcium magnesium carbonate), sometimes suggested because of its low price.

Live sand is also a substrate option (see page 82),

Leveled, equipped, filled, aquascaped, cycled, and ready for stocking: having the system running well before adding fishes prevents many typical new tank problems and losses.

although most new aquarium owners setting up fish-only systems will be perfectly well served by using a basic, dry coral sand substrate.

Once a substrate choice is made, the next question is how much to purchase. Buy enough to create a bed approximately ½ to 1 inch deep, or roughly ¼ to ½ pound of dry substrate per gallon. This depth can be increased or decreased depending on the animals to be kept. If wrasses, gobies, or other burrowing fishes will be housed in the tank, it may be necessary to create a deeper substrate bed. However, if large predators that produce heavy wastes will be showcased in the aquarium, it is preferable to use a shallower substrate layer so that the detritus produced can more readily be vacuumed out.

CHAPTER 5

SELECTING FISHES

A Guide to Stocking a Marine Community Tank

IN THE WILD, MANY MARINE FISHES FAVORED by aquarists are extremely territorial, defending their patch of the reef against all comers. Others, while not necessarily territorial, are active piscivores—fishes that live by eating other, smaller fishes. And some species are so attuned to their particular reef habitats or food sources that they often perish in captivity.

How to know which is which?

For many new hobbyists, deciding among the hundreds of species commonly found in aquarium shops is both exciting and bewildering. Unfortunately, buying the wrong fish or combination of fishes is commonplace. To save wasted dollars and to prevent the unnecessary loss of specimens, it helps to make some basic choices before actually purchasing even a single fish. Knowing the type

Left: the Yellow Tang (*Zebrasoma flavescens*) is a favorite among marine aquarists. **Above:** selecting fishes from a retail display.

of community your aquarium will house, or what the focal point species will be, can greatly help in making decisions about all livestock additions.

BALANCING ACT

THERE IS ONE TRUTH that escapes many beginning aquarists: a tank of healthy, "happy" fishes is much, much more enjoyable to watch and keep than one where there are constant battles, torn fins, and stressed, wasting or disappearing individuals.

This chapter is an attempt to present the very best choices for new aquarists and to help the newcomer avoid the same stocking mistakes that so many others of us have made. I visualize the three key elements in choosing fishes as three interconnected qualities:

Aggressiveness & Size

Because of the territorial nature of most marine fishes, choosing which species to place together in an aquarium first involves matching the degree of aggressiveness of the fishes chosen as well as their size.

For example, damselfishes are small, but ounce for ounce, they are as feisty as any fishes on the reef. By virtue of their scrappy nature, they are generally not good tankmates for small, meeker reef fishes like cardinalfishes or gobies, but they can hold their own with many other aggressive species, including many larger fishes. However, they do not mix well with large, predatory lionfishes or groupers, which can readily make a meal of the damsels; their scrappiness means nothing to a single-minded hunter with a gaping maw.

When considering what fishes to place in a saltwater system, I like to group the choices into one of these four categories:

- Slow-aggressive
- Fast-aggressive
- Moderately aggressive
- Docile

Slow-aggressive types include the large predatory fishes, notably many of the groupers, lionfishes, moray eels, and others.

Fast-aggressive fishes, in my scheme, are not often predatory on their tankmates but can be very tough when competing for food or space. Such fishes include triggerfishes, large tangs, large angelfishes, and large wrasses.

A considerable number of the fishes kept by marine aquarists are **moderately aggressive**. This group includes dwarf angelfishes, dottybacks, most wrasses, hawkfishes, damselfishes, and others. (Some of these are very quick, but are grouped here because they are smaller and tend to defer to the larger fishes in the previous group.)

The **docile** group includes fishes that are, for the most part, nonbelligerent and feed in a slow, nonaggressive manner. Not well suited to close competition for food in an aquarium, these fishes should only be housed with nonaggressive tankmates. Members of this group include mandarinfishes, firefishes, jawfishes, small gobies, and others. The Temperament Chart (page 89) lists my ranking of many of the popular families of marine fishes and their relative aggressiveness.

The time-tested rule is to avoid mixing extremes (large with small, aggressive with nonaggressive) in community aquariums. Decide early whether you prefer a tank of small, docile, colorful fishes, a system with a few big, rugged personalities, or even a tank that displays a single species (see Starter Aquariums, page 99).

Generally speaking, fishes from one group in the chart do better with other members from that group, although they can be mixed with members from one group above or below. (Again, docile fishes that don't compete well for food and space with more aggressive species are generally best kept only with other docile tankmates.)

Some families contain members that fit into more than one group. (For example, some dottybacks can be fast-aggressive, such as the Australian Dottyback [*Ogilbyina novaehollandiae*]; others are just moderately aggressive, such as the *Pseudochromis* species). These groupings, therefore, are somewhat arbitrary but are constructed to provide a template for trying to match fishes of like temperaments. There are many exceptions, and it should be noted that occasionally an individual of a docile group will exhibit a case of extremely aberrant behavior: e.g., a goby that attacks all of its tankmates. Therefore good judgment and careful observation need to be exercised even when the group's behavior is thought to be known. When purchasing a new specimen, always investigate its aggressiveness, potential size, and its likely compatibility with your existing collection of fishes.

Hardiness

Hardiness in gardening is a fairly technical term, with a given plant usually described as hardy within certain geographical zones or a set range of temperatures.

> "To save wasted dollars and to prevent the unnecessary loss of specimens, it helps to make some basic choices before actually purchasing even a single fish."
>
> ■ ■ ■

Marine fishes are commonly given hardiness ratings based on a much larger set of variables: ability to recover from collection and shipping stresses; adaptability to aquarium conditions; willingness to accept prepared foods; and survivability in adverse circumstances. The new aquarist has a much greater chance of success with specimens generally regarded as "hardy" or "durable." (Ask knowledgeable aquarists, aquarium-store staff or consult a good reference on coral reef fishes.)

STOCKING LEVELS

IN ADDITION TO CHOOSING a combination of fishes that are compatible with each other, it is also very important not to overstock the aquarium. That is, even if a good grouping of fishes is chosen, the filtration system must be able to handle the amount of waste produced, or the tank will fail. In aquariums equipped with an undergravel filter and decorated with dead coral, this was a significant problem. Fortunately, the live rock/protein skimmer methodology allows a greater number of fishes to be kept before the biological filter becomes overtaxed. The problem more likely to occur in this system is aggression among the fishes—also a result of stocking errors—rather than inadequate filtration capacity.

The old rule of thumb for stocking a saltwater system was 1 inch of fish per 5 gallons of water. This is a rough and arbitrary rule that is often ignored for the simple reason that it doesn't always make sense: one 5-inch grouper would produce significantly more waste than five 1-inch damselfishes. A live rock system has a much more generous margin of error in its stocking limits. I will suggest a loose guideline of 1 inch of fish per 2 gallons of water. Obviously, the fewer fish per gallon the greater the margin of safety.

Still, every aquarium has its limits. If a tank is overpopulated, something—disease or aggression leading to the death of weaker specimens—will occur to bring the fish numbers and biological capacity of the system into balance. Even if the aquarium seems fine during normal operation, an overstocked system will crash much faster in the event of a power failure. Overstocking is a recipe for trouble, and the ecosystem you have created, no matter how large or small, will eventually experience problems due to overpopulation. Clearly, it is always better

TEMPERAMENT CHART
KEY: 1 = Slow-Aggressive   2 = Fast-Aggressive
3 = Moderately Aggressive   4 = Docile

Group	Temperament Range
SLOW-AGGRESSIVE (generally large)	
Frogfishes	1
Groupers	1
Lionfishes	1
Moray Eels	1, 2
True Puffers	1
Porcupinefishes	1
FAST-AGGRESSIVE (generally large)	
Triggerfishes	2
Angelfishes	2, 3
Damselfishes	2, 3
Squirrelfishes	2, 3
Surgeonfishes (Tangs)	2, 3
Dottybacks	2, 3, 4
Wrasses	2, 3, 4
MODERATELY AGGRESSIVE (generally med./sm.)	
Rabbitfishes	3
Sweetlips	3
Tobies	3
Anthias	3, 4
Blennies	3, 4
Butterflyfishes	3, 4
Clownfishes	3, 4
Grammas	3, 4
Comet (Marine Betta)	3, 4
DOCILE (generally small)	
Cardinalfishes	4
Gobies	4
Jawfishes	4

to keep the fish density within reasonable limits.

New aquarists generally have to learn this lesson the hard way. Adding too many specimens or choosing fishes that grow to overwhelm the size of the tank are very common mistakes. Since it is not the goal of keeping a successful marine tank to be replacing dead fishes constantly, we all need to exercise some discipline and avoid the persistent temptation to add "just one more fish."

FISHES FOR BEGINNERS

ALMOST ANY MARINE FISH whose dietary and space requirements can easily be met with standard foods and a reasonable-sized aquarium can be considered a good fish for the beginning hobbyist. However, some fish families are easier to acclimate and are more tolerant of captivity than others. Because few beginners have tanks over 100 gallons, most of the larger species will have to wait. While many of these fishes are available as juveniles and will generally do quite well while small, they eventually outgrow their tanks. If initially housed with small fishes, the day may very well come when they start to consume their tankmates. I strongly urge you not to purchase a potentially large fish—certain groupers, sharks, eels, large angelfishes, and triggerfishes come to mind—if it is going to outgrow your tank and you don't have a future home ready and waiting. (Public aquariums will usually refuse offers of overgrown fishes, but some retail pet shops will take back large, healthy fishes "on consignment." Ask about their policy before buying. In many cases, the aquarist will not recoup the original price of the fish and will simply end up grateful to have found the animal a new home.)

Fortunately, there are hundreds of attractive and hardy reef fishes that remain relatively small. The list-ings that follow in this chapter represent some of the best choices for a beginning saltwater aquarist. (Some of the groups listed, such as seahorses and pipefishes, have no species recommended for beginners. They are included here because they are often tempting to new aquarists, but because of their special-care requirements, they should be avoided until a more advanced level of fish-keeping expertise is reached.)

Obviously, there are many other appropriate species, but those listed below represent a starting selection of attractive fishes that are commonly available and that have proved to be hardy survivors for many aquarists.

MORAY EELS
Family Muraenidae

MORAY EELS ARE HARDY, fascinating fishes that can do well, even under a beginner's care. Unfortunately, many species grow much too large for most aquariums. Even the common Snowflake Moray (*Echidna nebulosa*), which is often available in small sizes, will outgrow the average first aquarium in a few years. (The eel itself may do fine in a tank as small as 30 to 40 gallons, but it will be too much for a community tank of this size.) For the short term, an eel makes an interesting addition, but be prepared to move it or step up to a larger system when it starts to mature. (Be sure to investigate the growth potential of any eel species you may be considering.)

Moray eels generally have poor eyesight but a superior sense of smell, so in a tank they need to be fed directly, otherwise the faster fishes in the tank will out-

Whitemouth Moray (*Gymnothorax meleagris*): a handsome aquarium species, but one that will outgrow smaller tanks.

Snowflake Moray (*Echidna nebulosa*): an excellent and justifiably popular beginner's eel, being easy to keep and readily available.

Longspine Squirrelfish (*Holocentrus rufus*): will eat ornamental shrimps.

Blackbar Soldierfish (*Myripristis jacobus*): provide a cave or rocky overhang.

Hawaiian Squirrelfish (*Sargocentron xantherythrum*): may be kept in groups.

compete them for food. The best method is to spear a piece of shrimp or squid on a feeding stick and place it near the eel's lair or wiggle it until the eel emerges to take the item. (Hand-feeding is not recommended.)

A tank housing moray eels must be completely sealed—these agile animals will escape through even the smallest opening, only to dry up and die on the floor. (Such eels will sometimes rebound, even when apparently dead, if returned to the water in time.)

Recommended species (choose juvenile individuals): Snowflake Moray (*Echidna nebulosa*); Whitemouth Moray (*Gymnothorax meleagris)*; Whitelip Moray (*Gymnothorax chilospilus*); Jewel Moray (*Muraena lentiginosa*).

SQUIRRELFISHES & SOLDIERFISHES
Family Holocentridae

LARGE EYES and red coloration suggest the nocturnal habits of these fishes. Unless adequate caves and hiding places are provided, squirrelfishes and soldierfishes will generally not do well. With the right environment, however, they will acclimate to captivity quickly, although they will always tend to be shy except at feeding time.

The squirrelfishes and soldierfishes will rapidly adapt to eating chunks of fleshy food as it passes by their hiding places. These fishes will also consume any tankmate (small fishes, shrimps, or crabs) that they can swallow whole, so some consideration of size should be made when selecting their tankmates.

Recommended species: Longspine Squirrelfish (*Holocentrus rufus*); Crown Squirrelfish (*Sargocentron diadema*); Redcoat Squirrelfish (*Sargocentron rubrum*); Hawaiian Squirrelfish (*Sargocentron xantherythrum*); Blackbar Soldierfish (*Myripristis jacobus*); Violet Soldierfish (*Myripristis violacea*); Whitetip Soldierfish (*Myripristis vittata*).

SEAHORSES & PIPEFISHES
Family Syngnathidae

ALTHOUGH SOLD TO CHILDREN for keeping in bowls, seahorses must be fed frequently with live foods, such as adult brine shrimp, and they do very poorly when kept with most reef fishes. In addition, seahorses are under tremendous worldwide pressure from habitat destruction and harvest for Oriental folk medicine. Both seahorses and pipefishes should be left to more advanced aquarists willing to devote a species tank and extra attention to their care. When available, captive-propagated specimens will be the best choice for interested aquarists.

Recommended species: None (should be kept by experienced aquarists only).

LIONFISHES
Family Scorpaenidae

THE LIONFISHES, with their elaborate finnage and the mystique of their array of venomous spines, are among the most fascinating groups of fishes available to the marine aquarist.

Several species are quite hardy and are not pugnacious, despite their defensive stinging abilities. They will only bother smaller fishes and ornamental shrimps that they can swallow whole; otherwise they leave their tankmates alone. The biggest challenge is in picking a species whose adult size will match the tank in which it is to be placed. Fortunately, lionfish species range significantly in size, so one can be selected to fit in just about any tank.

These fishes usually start out needing to be offered live foods. They should be weaned from this to fresh or frozen seafood as quickly as possible so that a more nutritious diet can be provided. To do this, a chunk of food should be agitated in the water (on a feeding stick—

Zebra Lionfish (*Dendrochirus zebra*): one of the relatively small lionfish species and often sold as the Dwarf Lionfish.

Spotfin Lionfish (*Pterois antennata*): hardy species of modest size, but with the venomous spines common to all in this group.

never with bare hands) to mimic live food. Doing this while providing food that is highly aromatic, such as squid or shrimp, is usually enough to entice them to eat. Care should be taken not to overfeed lionfishes as this results in their liver becoming fatty, ultimately causing their demise. (The regular use of live feeder goldfish is not recommended, as it can lead to health problems and death.)

Always use caution when handling a lionfish or working in its tank. (If you are stung, place the wound under hot—but not scalding—running water to detoxify the venom. Seek medical care immediately if symptoms other than localized pain develop.)

Recommended species: Hardy lionfishes that stay relatively small are the Hawaiian Lionfish (*Pterois sphex*), Spotfin Lionfish (*Pterois antennata*), and the Zebra Lionfish (*Dendrochirus zebra*). The Volitans Lionfish (*Pterois volitans*) and Russell's Lionfish (*Pterois russelli*)—also sold as the Red Volitans—are also excellent choices, but will outgrow a small aquarium and will eat smaller, slower tankmates, such as clownfishes.

GROUPERS
Family Serranidae — Tribe Epinephelini

THE GROUPERS ARE THE BIG PUPPY DOGS of the marine hobby. Many of these marine basses reach large sizes and can fill entire tanks if they are fed well. Big groupers will swallow any fish that they can—sometimes with blinding speed—even if the victim is as much as two-thirds the size of the grouper itself, so care should be exercised in choosing their tankmates. The tank should be

Coral Hind or Miniata Grouper (*Cephalopholis miniata*): gaudy and popular, but a predatory species that often stays hidden.

Coney (*Cephalopholis fulva*): an attractive Caribbean grouper with several color phases, including red, brown, bicolor, and golden.

aquascaped to provide rocky hiding places, although many aquarists are disappointed to find that a grouper will naturally spend most of its time lurking in caves or under overhangs rather than swimming in the open.

Feeding these fishes is not a problem once they have become acclimated, as they will eat any large fleshy pieces of food they can swallow. Chunks of shrimp or fish are readily accepted as are occasional treats of live feeder fish. Care should be taken not to overfeed these fishes—they tend to develop fatty livers and die. Feeder goldfish should not be overused as they tend to be of poor nutritional value. (Many aquarists avoid the use of feeder goldfish altogether, as it may increase the aggressiveness

of predators like lionfishes, eels, and groupers.)

Before buying any of these larger-growing groupers, consider that their size, predatory behavior, and waste-generating abilities will greatly limit the types and numbers of other fishes you might want to place in the same tank. (As alternatives, consider some of the smaller seabasses and grouper relatives, such as the grammas, basslets, and the Comet [*Calloplesiops altivelis*].)

Recommended species: Panther Grouper (*Cromileptes altivelis*); Coral Hind or Miniata Grouper (*Cephalopholis miniata*); V-tailed Hind, Flagtail Grouper, or Darkfin Hind (*Cephalopholis urodeta*); Coney (*Cephalopholis fulva*).

TWENTY-FOUR GREAT SPECIES FOR NEW AQUARISTS

- Snowflake Moray (*Echidna nebulosa*)
- Volitans Lionfish (*Pterois volitans*)
- Chalk Bass (*Serranus tortugarum*)
- Orchid Dottyback (*Pseudochromis fridmani*)
- Royal Gramma (*Gramma loreto*)
- Comet (Marine Betta) (*Calloplesiops altivelis*)
- Longnose Hawkfish (*Oxycirrhites typus*)
- Flame Hawkfish (*Neocirrhites armatus*)
- Banggai Cardinalfish (*Pterapogon kauderni*)
- Pajama Cardinalfish (*Sphaeramia nematoptera*)
- Coral Beauty Angelfish (*Centropyge bispinosa*)
- Flame Angelfish (*Centropyge loricula*)

- Yellowtail Damselfish (*Chrysiptera parasema*)
- Ocellaris Clownfish (*Amphiprion ocellaris*)
- Clark's Clownfish (*Amphiprion clarkii*)
- Golden or Canary Wrasse (*Halichoeres chrysus*)
- Sixline Wrasse (*Pseudocheilinus hexataenia*)
- Bicolor Blenny (*Ecsenius bicolor*)
- Neon Goby (*Gobiosoma oceanops*)
- Firefish (*Nemateleotris magnifica*)
- Foxface (*Siganus vulpinus*)
- Yellow Tang (*Zebrasoma flavescens*)
- Yellowtail Blue (Hippo) Tang (*Paracanthurus hepatus*)
- Picasso Triggerfish (*Rhinecanthus aculeatus*)

Chalk Bass (*Serranus tortugarum*): one of several Caribbean dwarf seabasses highly recommended for beginners' tanks.

Harlequin Bass (*Serranus tigrinus*): more active and much better suited to smaller aquariums than any of the full-sized groupers.

DWARF SEABASSES
Family Serranidae — Genus *Serranus*

VERY MUCH GROUPERLIKE, with self-assured personalities and predatory instincts, the dwarf seabasses include some very attractive species that never exceed a relatively modest size. They hail from the Western Atlantic and Caribbean and do particularly well in live rock aquariums with ample hiding places. The attractive little Chalk Bass should be kept in pairs or groups, while the more aggressive species will fare better singly, unless a mated pair is purchased.

Recommended species: Chalk Bass (*Serranus tortugarum*); Orangeback Bass (*Serranus annularis*); Lantern Bass (*Serranus baldwini*); Harlequin Bass (*Serranus tigrinus*).

ANTHIAS
Family Serranidae — Subfamily Anthiinae

ALTHOUGH BEAUTIFUL AND PLENTIFUL, the many species of anthias do not include any that make especially good choices for new aquarium keepers. Anthias demand frequent feeding and most are highly territorial toward members of their own species—and other anthias.

Recommended species: None. (Care by an experienced aquarist required.)

GRAMMAS & REEF BASSLETS
Families Grammatidae & Serranidae

THE GRAMMAS AND REEF BASSLETS belong to two groups of related fishes, mostly found in the tropical Western Atlantic and Caribbean, that have been kept in aquariums since the beginning of modern marine fishkeeping. Their bright colors, hardy nature, and interesting behaviors make them the perfect choice for beginning aquarists. The most frequently encountered member of this group is the Royal Gramma (*Gramma loreto*). More than one specimen of this species can be kept in a tank as long as adequate hiding places are provided. Placing two or more juveniles or individuals of different sizes may help reduce aggression—the males are noticeably larger, and one male for two females is a good

Royal Gramma (*Gramma loreto*): a perfect species for new marine aquarists.

Swissguard Basslet (*Liopropoma rubre*): a prized but elusive and pricey species.

Blackcap Basslet (*Gramma melacara*): a good choice from deeper waters.

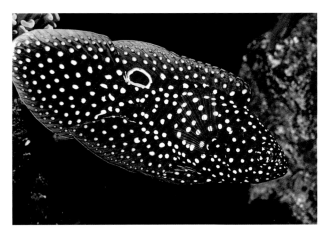

Comet (*Calloplesiops altivelis*): known to some as the Marine Betta, this is a somewhat shy but much-liked aquarium fish.

Blue Assessor (*Assessor macneilli*): not always available, but an eye-catching species that requires rocky caves and refuges.

ratio. These fish show a tendency to have their colors fade over time in captivity. To reduce this possibility, they need to be fed a varied diet containing a large percentage of shrimp or other marine crustacean meat.

Two once-rare grammas, the Blackcap Basslet (*Gramma melacara*) and the somewhat more aggressive Brazilian Gramma (*Gramma* sp.) are becoming more available, but at a higher price than the Royal Gramma.

Also expensive to acquire are members of the genus *Liopropoma*, the most commonly seen species being the Swissguard or Peppermint Basslet (*Liopropoma rubre*). Extremely adept at avoiding capture, these reef basslets command high prices and are only sporadically available. Given a home with live rock for cover and no large, hostile tankmates, they make great aquarium specimens.
Recommended species: Royal Gramma (*Gramma loreto*); Blackcap Basslet (*Gramma melacara*); Brazilian Gramma (*Gramma* sp.); Swissguard Basslet (*Liopropoma rubre*).

COMET & ASSESSORS
Family Plesiopidae
THE CRYPTIC COMET (sometimes sold as the Marine Betta) and the small, colorful assessors do well in most tanks as long as adequate caves and hiding places are present. Unfortunately, these fishes will spend much of their time in caves or under overhangs. This is particularly true of the Comet. Despite this shortcoming, the sudden appearance of this white polka-dotted beauty still makes it a worthwhile aquarium choice.

In tanks with more competitive fishes, care must be taken to ensure that these fishes do not starve. Rather than simply adding food to the tank, the aquarist must direct some meaty pieces toward the places where these fishes are hiding.
Recommended species: Comet (*Calloplesiops altivelis*); Yellow Assessor (*Assessor flavissimus*); Blue Assessor (*Assessor macneilli*).

JAWFISHES
Family Opistognathidae
ALTHOUGH LACKING THE BRILLIANT COLORS of many coral reef fishes, members of the jawfish family offer interesting additions to a marine aquarium because of their burrowing behavior. If the substrate is deep enough and of the right consistency, these fishes will excavate a tunnel or series of tunnels in which to live.

In a display tank, special arrangements may need to

FISH OR FISHES?

Newcomers to fish circles are often guilty of misusing the basic terms *fish* and *fishes*. *Fish*, of course, can mean a single specimen, but it can also be used for a group of specimens of the same species. (For example: "Those Percula Clowns are beautiful fish.") When speaking of a number of specimens including more than one species, the proper term is *fishes*. (For example: "My favorite fishes are the marine angels.")

Yellowhead Jawfish (*Opistognathus aurifrons*): a fascinating burrower that should be provided a deep bed of substrate.

be made if jawfishes are to be kept successfully. The substrate will need to be at least 4 inches deep in at least one portion of the aquarium, and a flat stone should be placed over part of this area. When such conditions are available, the jawfish will usually dig out a cavern with the flat rock serving as a roof, providing the fish with the secure home it seems to need in order to thrive in a captive setting.

Recommended species: Yellowhead Jawfish (*Opistognathus aurifrons*); Dusky Jawfish (*Opistognathus whitehursti*).

DOTTYBACKS
Family Pseudochromidae

DESPITE THEIR RELATIVELY SMALL SIZES, some of the pseudochromids pack a considerable level of aggressiveness. After the damselfishes, a number of dottybacks have more pugnacity inch for inch than virtually any other commonly kept marine family. Despite this, and because of their hardy survivability and bright coloration, these fishes are welcome additions to most tanks if some rules for housing them are followed.

Their aggressive tendencies are often exhibited against other members of their family as well as other similarly shaped fishes, such as wrasses and assessors. They also tend to resent any fishes added to the aquarium once they have staked out their own territories. The largest members of this family are the ones likely to do the most damage. To avoid problems, only one individual of the more aggressive dottyback genera should be kept per tank, and it should be one of the last fishes added. Other like-shaped fishes should be kept to a minimum, and the largest members of this group should be acquired only if the aquarium is a large one (over 90 gallons). In addition, the scrappier dottybacks should only be housed with other aggressive fishes.

Springer's Dottyback (*Pseudochromis springeri*): good, less aggressive choice.

Orchid Dottyback (*Pseudochromis fridmani*): vivid, less aggressive choice.

Sankey's Dottyback (*Pseudochromis sankeyi*): nice, less aggressive choice.

Neon Dottyback (*Pseudochromis aldabraensis*): feisty and best kept singly.

Bicolor Dottyback (*Pseudochromis paccagnellae*): small but scrappy species.

Sunrise Dottyback (*Pseudochromis flavivertex*): will battle other dottybacks.

Recommended species: The best choices are three less pugnacious species: the Orchid Dottyback (*Pseudochromis fridmani*); Springer's Dottyback (*Pseudochromis springeri*); and Sankey's (Black-and-White) Dottyback (*Pseudochromis sankeyi*). If a large enough tank is provided and they are introduced together, it is possible to house two or more specimens of a given species together. Other small but scrappier species include the Neon Dottyback (*Pseudochromis aldabraensis*); Sunrise Dottyback (*Pseudochromis flavivertex*); Bicolor Dottyback (*Pseudochromis paccagnellae*); and Purple Dottyback (*Pseudochromis porphyreus*). These should be kept one individual to a tank.

Species to avoid: members of the genera *Ogilbyina* and *Labracinus*—such as the Australian Dottyback (*Ogilbyina novaehollandiae*); the Sailfin Dottyback (*Ogilbyina velifera*); and the Red Dottyback (*Labracinus cyclophthalmus*)—are large, fierce, and capable of terrorizing an entire tank.

home tanks by many hobbyists without special equipment. (In this one species, the male incubates both the eggs and fry in its mouth. The young are large enough to accept newly hatched brine shrimp as soon as they are free-swimming.)

Most cardinalfishes are easy to keep as long as hiding places are provided where they can feel secure. Feeding is also simple as long as meaty foods, such as chopped shrimp or squid, as well as frozen plankton are provided. Some species form large schools, others stay in smaller aggregations, and still others are solitary. In the species that form groups, fighting among individuals is usually limited to small squabbles, but others will battle if crowded without adequate hiding places.

Recommended species: Banggai or Highfin Cardinalfish (*Pterapogon kauderni*); Pajama Cardinalfish (*Sphaeramia nematoptera*); Flamefish (*Apogon maculatus*); Orangestriped Cardinalfish (*Apogon cyanosoma*).

CARDINALFISHES
Family Apogonidae

THIS LARGE FAMILY of small carnivorous fishes has members in every tropical ocean. One fascinating behavioral fact is that they are mouthbrooders: the male incubates and guards the eggs in his mouth. Because of its unusual reproductive traits, the Banggai Cardinalfish (*Pterapogon kauderni*), has now been bred and raised in

BUTTERFLYFISHES
Family Chaetodontidae

Recommended species: None. (In my experience, none of the butterflyfishes should be considered a good beginner's fish. Once the aquarist has some confidence in keeping reef fishes, butterflyfish choices could include some of the hardier species like the Longfin Bannerfish (*Heniochus acuminatus*); Raccoon Butterflyfish (*Chaetodon*

Pajama Cardinalfish (*Sphaeramia nematoptera*): a hardy, quiet species.

Orangestriped Cardinalfish (*Apogon cyanosoma*): may be kept in groups.

Banggai or Highfin Cardinal (*Pterapogon kauderni*): easily bred in captivity.

lunula); Threadfin Butterflyfish (*Chaetodon auriga*); and Yellow Longnose Butterflyfish (*Forcipiger flavissimus*).

ANGELFISHES
Family Pomacanthidae

ONE OF THE MOST POPULAR marine fish groups, owing to their beautiful colors and bold behaviors, is the angelfish family. These fishes can be generalized into three groups, roughly based on size:

- Large (genera *Holacanthus* and *Pomacanthus*)
- Medium (genera *Chaetodontoplus* and *Genicanthus*)
- Small (genus *Centropyge*)

There are several other angelfish genera—among them some of the most beautiful of all marine fishes—but these should be avoided by the beginning hobbyist as their members typically do not do well without exceptional care. Even many advanced hobbyists cannot keep them successfully. These include *Pygoplites*, *Apolemichthys*, and the subgenus *Euxiphipops*.

The ease with which angelfishes can be kept is often related to their dietary requirements. Many of the large species do not do well because their food in the wild consists mainly of live sponges and cannot be duplicated in the aquarium setting. When buying any of the larger angelfish species, it is highly advisable to wait for a good, healthy juvenile and raise it on a diet that is not sponge-derived. Their diet should include both high-quality protein of marine origin and a high percentage of vegetable matter, crucial to keeping them successfully. Some frozen angelfish rations now contain edible sponge, and some species will relish an occasional meal of this food.

Never introduce an angelfish into a new aquarium.

French Angelfish (*Pomacanthus paru*): very hardy Caribbean species, but one demanding a large (at least 6-foot-long) system.

Half Moon Angelfish (*Pomacanthus maculosus*): a rugged Red Sea species that will quickly outgrow smaller aquariums.

Coral Beauty Angelfish (*Centropyge bispinosa*): like others in this group, best added only to a tank that has run for several months.

Flame Angelfish (*Centropyge loricula*): highly prized dwarf angel that does well in established tanks aquascaped with live rock.

FISH CHOICES FOR FIVE STARTER AQUARIUMS

There are, needless to say, many fishes in the sea, and the following suggestions
are offered simply as starting points for the new aquarist to plan his or her first collection of species.
Try to balance sizes, temperaments, activity levels, and colors for a successful and pleasing mix of fishes.

Stocking guide: 1 inch of fish per 2 gallons of tank volume

40-GALLON PEACEFUL COMMUNITY TANK

❏ 1 pair Ocellaris Clownfish (*Amphiprion ocellaris*)

❏ 2 Pajama Cardinalfish (*Sphaeramia nematoptera*)

❏ 1 to 2 Firefish (*Nemateleotris magnifica*)

OR 2 to 3 Neon Gobies (*Gobiosoma oceanops*)

❏ 1 shrimp goby (e.g. *Cryptocentrus* or
Amblyeleotris spp.) with commensal snapping
shrimp (*Alpheus* spp.), if available

Note: A 36-inch-long tank will suffice for this collection
of docile but colorful and interesting fishes.

40-TO-50-GALLON MIXED COMMUNITY TANK

❏ 3 to 5 Yellowtail Damselfishes (*Chrysiptera
parasema*)

OR 1 to 2 Golden or Canary Wrasses
(*Halichoeres chrysus*)

❏ 1 Flame Angelfish (*Centropyge loricula*)

OR 1 Flame Hawkfish (*Neocirrhites armatus*)

❏ 1 Midas Blenny (*Ecsenius midas*)

OR 1 Lawnmower Blenny (*Salarias fasciatus*)

❏ 1 small Foxface Rabbitfish (*Siganus vulpinus*)

OR 1 small Yellow Tang (*Zebrasoma flavescens*)

Note: A 40-gallon "long" tank (48-inch length) is
required to accommodate a growing Foxface or tang.

55-TO-75-GALLON MIXED COMMUNITY TANK

❏ 1 to 2 Yellowtail Blue (Hippo) Tangs (*Paracanthurus hepatus*)

❏ 5 to 7 Blue Green Chromis (*Chromis viridis*)

❏ 1 Coral Beauty Angelfish (*Centropyge bispinosa*)

❏ 1 Longnose Hawkfish (*Oxycirrhites typus*)

❏ 2 to 3 Banggai Cardinalfish (*Pterapogon kauderni*)

Note: The Yellowtail Blue Tangs suggested will coexist
in this system, but most other surgeonfish or tang
species should be kept singly to avoid fighting.

70-TO-90-GALLON CARIBBEAN COMMUNITY

❏ 1 Cherub Angelfish (*Centropyge argi*)

❏ 2 adult Royal Grammas (*Gramma loreto*)
OR 2 Blackcap Basslets (*Gramma melacara*)

❏ 2 Flamefish (*Apogon maculatus*)

❏ 1 to 2 Blackbar Soldierfish (*Myripristis jacobus*)

❏ 3 Chalk Bass (*Serranus tortugarum*)

Optional additions:

❏ 1 Spotfin Hogfish (*Bodianus pulchellus*)

❏ 1 Swissguard Basslet (*Liopropoma rubre*)

Note: This collection takes a simplified biotope
approach, with all species from the same general
geographic area. Provide caves and some coral rubble
to allow these fishes to display their natural behaviors.

120-GALLON PREDATOR/AGGRESSIVE TANK

❏ 1 Volitans Lionfish (*Pterois volitans*)
OR 1 Zebra Lionfish (*Dendrochirus zebra*)

❏ 1 Picasso Triggerfish (*Rhinecanthus aculeatus*)
OR 1 Redtooth (Niger) Triggerfish (*Odonus niger*)

❏ 1 Arc-eye Hawkfish (*Paracirrhites arcatus*)

❏ 1 Purple Tang (*Zebrasoma xanthurum*)
OR 1 Yellow Tang (*Zebrasoma flavescens*)

Optional additions:

❏ 1 V-tailed Hind/Grouper (*Cephalopholis urodeta*)

❏ 1 moray eel (Family Muraenidae)
e.g., Snowflake Moray (*Echidna nebulosa*) or
Zebra Moray (*Gymnomuraena zebra*)

Note: This collection includes aggressive and large-
growing species, some of which may eventually
demand more space. In planning for a system with an
eel, the usual stocking rules based on the body length
of fishes can be relaxed somewhat to accommodate
the moray's elongate body plan and generally
sedentary habits.

Redspotted Hawkfish (*Amblycirrhitus pinos*): attractive little species and the lone hawkfish from Caribbean waters.

Longnose Hawkfish (*Oxycirrhites typus*): excellent aquarium fish, but well able to attack and swallow small fishes and shrimps.

Freckled Hawkfish (*Paracirrhites forsteri*): a perching species, like all of the hawkfishes, ever-vigilant for passing food targets.

Arc-eye Hawkfish (*Paracirrhites arcatus*): a tough, popular species for systems with larger and more aggressive tankmates.

If placed in a system that is well established and offers natural grazing opportunities, its chances of adapting and settling in for a long life are much higher. If keeping one of the medium or small angelfishes, it is very important to have a body of established live rock to provide suitable foraging grounds. (Without live rock, many angels tend to decline and eventually perish.)

Angelfishes do best when not housed with other members of the same genus, as fighting will usually occur with one fish completely dominating the others. One marine angelfish per tank is an old but prudent rule for all but large aquariums. If an angelfish appears timid and hides all the time, some dither fish, like a school of small chromis, may be added to make it feel more secure. **Recommended species: Large:** French Angelfish (*Pomacanthus paru*); Koran Angelfish (*Pomacanthus semicirc-* *ulatus*); Half Moon Angelfish (*Pomacanthus maculosus*). **Medium:** Lamarck's Angelfish (*Genicanthus lamarck*); Blackspot Angelfish (*Genicanthus melanospilos*). **Small:** Flame Angelfish (*Centropyge loricula*); Coral Beauty Angelfish (*Centropyge bispinosa*); Cherub Angelfish (*Centropyge argi*).

HAWKFISHES
Family Cirrhitidae

THE HAWKFISHES are an interesting group, so named because of their habit of perching atop a piece of coral or live rock and swooping off it to capture food or prey as it passes by. This behavior is linked to their lack of a swim bladder, which prevents them from hovering in the water column for any length of time.

Hawkfishes come in a range of colors and sizes, and

Black-axil Chromis (*Chromis atripectoralis*): forms attractive schools.

Blue Damselfish (*Chrysiptera cyanea*): mature males often sport orange tails.

Behn's Damselfish (*Neoglyphidodon nigroris*): bright juvenile colors will fade.

some grow large enough to pose a real threat to small fishes, shrimps, crabs, and snails. Best kept singly, a hawkfish needs to be fed meaty foods and should be provided with an area where it can perch. Although the hawkfish is not an active swimmer, its ever-alert eyes and ability to dart out to capture food with great agility will make it an interesting, likable tank inhabitant.

Recommended species (with less aggressive tankmates): Longnose Hawkfish (*Oxycirrhites typus*); Flame Hawkfish (*Neocirrhites armatus*); Redspotted Hawkfish (*Amblycirrhitus pinos*).

Recommend species (with more aggressive tankmates): Coral or Pixy Hawkfish (*Cirrhitichthys oxycephalus*); Arc-eye Hawkfish (*Paracirrhites arcatus*); Freckled Hawkfish (*Paracirrhites forsteri*);

> ### SELECTION TIP
> A typical fish will grow continuously during its life in the aquarium. While a tank may seem empty at first, the system will become more crowded as the fishes mature. Always stock with future growth in mind.
>
> ■ ■ ■

aggressive will harass and dominate all of the smaller ones. As a result, the smaller damsels will often have torn or ripped fins and be more susceptible to infections.

Damselfishes are usually sold at very small sizes, so their aggressive nature is often hidden. However, as they grow (and some do grow quite large) their true belligerence begins to come out. A good rule is to keep only one damselfish per tank—or else a group of four or more to spread the aggression. The exceptions are *Chromis* species, which should be kept in schools.

Recommended species: Blue Green Chromis (*Chromis viridis*) and the similar Black-axil Chromis (*Chromis atripectoralis*); Neon Damsel (*Pomacentrus coelestis*); Yellowbellied Damsel (*Pomacentrus caeruleus*); Yellowtail Damsel (*Chrysiptera parasema*); Blue Damsel (*Chrysiptera cyanea*); South Seas Devil Damsel (*Chrysiptera taupou*).

DAMSELFISHES
Family Pomacentridae

DAMSELFISHES are generally thought of as being the best first fishes for a new saltwater hobbyist. They are colorful, active, feed readily, and are very hardy. In fact they are so hardy, they are often used to "break in" a new tank, creating and then surviving the first waves of toxic ammonia.

Unfortunately, they are also some of the most territorial smaller fishes on the reef. If they are introduced first, they will harass many of the new fishes added after them. In the small confines of most aquariums, if more than one damselfish is introduced, the largest and most

CLOWNFISHES
Family Pomacentridae
Genus *Amphiprion* & Genus *Premnas*

THE CLOWNFISHES, which are members of the damselfish family, probably get more hobbyists interested in keeping a marine tank than any other fishes. The sight of a pair of clownfish frolicking in the stinging tentacles of a sea anemone is an image that has become synonymous with the coral reef. Fortunately, most of the available clownfishes are relatively easy to keep and can live contentedly in an aquarium for many years. Sadly, most of their host anemones are difficult to sustain without in-

Ocellaris Clownfish (*Amphiprion ocellaris*): great choice for a first marine aquarium.

Clark's Clownfish (*Amphiprion clarkii*): vividly striped and very easy to keep.

Pink Skunk Clownfish (*Amphiprion perideraion*): will thrive without a host anemone.

tense lighting, strong circulation, and expert care. Contrary to popular advice, clownfishes will thrive and even reproduce in a home tank without their host anemone being present.

Most clownfishes do best when kept either singly or in pairs. These fishes are protandrous hermaphrodites. They all start off as males, but as they grow and develop, the largest, most dominant fish will become a female. To get a pair established, two small clownfish of the same species should be introduced to the tank together. The slightly larger of the two will then develop into the female. In this pair, the female will be more aggressive in defending the territory and attacking other fish than will the male. The male acts predominantly to serve the female. (With the feisty Maroon Clownfish [*Premnas biaculeatus*], always place two individuals of unequal size together and be ready to remove one if severe fighting takes place. With luck, the larger fish should take over as the matriarch.) As an exception to the rule, Ocellaris (False Percula) Clownfish can be kept in groups, at least until pairs form and new homes must be found for the extras.

Clownfishes do not usually tolerate other clownfish species being present in their territory. Fight the temptation to keep several different species of clownfish together in one tank—the most aggressive species will usually kill off the less dominant types until only one species remains.

> ### SELECTION TIP
> Some larger fishes will act shy and hide in the presence of other large fishes. Introducing a group of four to six active, constantly moving "dither fish," such as Blue Green Chromis (*Chromis viridis*) or active wrasses will help bring some of these reluctant species out into the open parts of the aquarium more often.
>
> ■ ■ ■

Recommended species: Ocellaris Clownfish (*Amphiprion ocellaris*); Pink Skunk Clownfish (*Amphiprion perideraion*); Maroon Clownfish (*Premnas biaculeatus*); Tomato Clownfish (*Amphiprion frenatus*); Clark's Clownfish (*Amphiprion clarkii*). (Clark's Clownfish are often incorrectly labeled "Sebae Clownfish." The true Sebae Clownfish [*Amphiprion sebae*] is actually a rarely seen species.)

WRASSES
Family Labridae

THIS DIVERSE GROUP OF FISHES ranges in size from the diminutive Sixline Wrasse (*Pseudocheilinus hexataenia*) to the gigantic Napoleon or Humphead Wrasse (*Cheilinus undulatus*). As with their size, these fishes also differ markedly in terms of their adaptability to aquarium life. Fortunately, there are enough different members of this clan available that a suitable wrasse species can be found to fit in just about any size or type of tank. Many wrasses offered for sale are juveniles, so an understanding of how large the fish will get as an adult should be considered before a purchase is made.

In addition to their flamboyant colors, wrasses are active fishes with some interesting behaviors. Some wrasses bury themselves in the sand when they sleep or when frightened. If these wrasses are to be kept, they require a fine-grained deep substrate. A coarser substrate can damage the wrasse's mouth or skin, creating wounds that are susceptible to bacterial infections.

Sharpfinned Flasher Wrasse (*Paracheilinus angulatus*): for quiet tanks.

Spanish Hogfish (*Bodianus rufus*): great fish but will outgrow smaller tanks.

Coral Hogfish (*Bodianus mesothorax*): a flashy but easily kept and popular species.

Golden Wrasse (*Halichoeres chrysus*): hardy, bright, and modestly sized.

Bird Wrasse (*Gomphosus varius*): an eye-catching favorite for bigger systems.

Harlequin Tuskfish (*Choerodon fasciatus*): an unusual wrasse for the big-fishes tank.

Some wrasses excrete a mucous cocoon around themselves while they sleep. This may prevent their scent from revealing their position to nocturnal predators. Other wrasses spend much of their time cleaning parasites from the bodies of large fishes.

Most wrasses are predatory, so a diet of meaty frozen or fresh marine foods will keep them healthy. Wrasses are also almost constantly in motion, so it is obvious that they need to be fed frequently. While feeding is usually not a problem, many wrasses have difficulty adapting to captivity. A strong effort needs to be made to acclimate them gradually and slowly to their new surroundings if they are going to thrive.

Many larger wrasses make excellent members of aggressive, bigger-fish community tanks. Especially good for beginners are the hardy hogfishes, such as the Spanish Hogfish (*Bodianus rufus*), Cuban Hogfish (*Bodianus pulchellus*), and Diana's Hogfish (*Bodianus diana*).

Note that many large wrasses will attack small fishes, shrimps, crabs, and other reef invertebrates, and they are

therefore not suitable for inclusion in reef tanks.

Recommended species (for quiet community tanks): smaller *Halichoeres* species, such as the Golden or Canary Wrasse (*Halichoeres chrysus*) and the Lemon Meringue Wrasse (*Halichoeres leucoxanthus*); fairy wrasses (*Cirrhilabrus* spp.); and flasher wrasses (*Paracheilinus* spp.).

Recommended species (for larger, more aggressive tanks): Moon Wrasse (*Thalassoma lunare*); Sunset Wrasse (*Thalassoma lutescens*); other *Thalassoma* species; larger *Halichoeres* species; hogfishes (*Bodianus* spp.); bird wrasses (*Gomphosus* spp.); Harlequin Tuskfish (*Choerodon fasciatus*).

Species to avoid: tamarin wrasses (*Anampses* spp.), cleaner wrasses (*Labroides* spp.), and leopard wrasses (*Macropharyngodon* spp.).

PARROTFISHES
Family Scaridae

Recommended species: None. (Parrotfishes tend to tolerate confinement poorly. Experienced care and very large systems required.)

> **SELECTION TIP**
>
> Fishes vary in their aggressiveness. The least-aggressive should be added to a tank first to allow them to acclimate and establish their territories.
>
> ■ ■ ■

Lawnmower Blenny (*Salarias fasciatus*): will graze algae from aquarium substrates.

Bicolor Blenny (*Ecsenius bicolor*): droll, likable choice for quiet aquariums.

Redspotted Blenny (*Istiblennius chryso-spilos*): unusual blenny choices abound.

BLENNIES
Family Blenniidae

THE BLENNIES are a large family of fishes whose members spend most of their time perching or moving from space to space as they graze algae from the rock. Many of these fishes do not swim in the classic manner of species that move easily in the water column—their anatomy allows them to swim only short distances, making their swimming motion look more like hopping. The blennies can have a strong sense of territory and will defend a small area against all intruders, especially those of the same species. Keep one specimen per blenny species per tank.

Because of their relatively small size, blennies are well suited to home aquariums as long as they are provided with a cave or small nook to use as a home base. They also require a diet high in vegetable matter. In the wild, they spend most of their time grazing on algae. If adequate algae is not present in the tank, it may be necessary to supplement their diet with nori or *Spirulina* algae.

Recommended species: Bicolor Blenny (*Ecsenius bicolor*); Dusky Blenny (*Astrosalarias fuscus*); Lawnmower Blenny or Jewelled Rockskipper (*Salarias fasciatus*).

GOBIES & GOBYLIKE FISHES
Families Gobiidae, Microdesmidae & others

THE GOBIES COMPRISE THE LARGEST FAMILY of fishes in the sea. The wormfishes and dartfishes, often sold as gobies in the aquarium trade, are similar but are classified in the Family Microdesmidae, which includes the popular firefishes and gudgeons.

Members of this diverse grouping of small, often-colorful fishes are generally not aggressive to tankmates and acclimate well to captivity. For these reasons, they make good inhabitants for home systems—as long as their tankmates are not too aggressive and only one of each genus is kept per aquarium.

Because some gobies are extremely small, these fishes need to be fed foods of the appropriate size, such as grated shrimp. Adult brine shrimp and prawn eggs are

Firefish (*Nemateleotris magnifica*): these elegant fishes do well with plenty of rocky hiding places where they can dart to safety.

Purple Firefish (*Nemateleotris decora*): an attractive hovering species that should not be housed with aggressive tankmates.

FISHES FOR THE BEGINNER TO AVOID

Until the aquarist has gained experience, these choices are best left to more advanced hobbyists.

Rock Beauty Angelfish

(*Holacanthus tricolor*)

Emperor Angelfish

(*Pomacanthus imperator*)

Threadfin Butterflyfish

(*Chaetodon auriga*)

Angelfishes:

    Apolemichthys species: All

    Bandit (*Desmoholacanthus arcuatus*)

    Bicolor (*Centropyge bicolor*)

    Blueface (*Pomacanthus xanthometopon*)

    Emperor (*Pomacanthus imperator*)

    Majestic or Bluegirdled (*Pomacanthus navarchus*)

    Manybar (*Centropyge multifasciata*)

    Regal (*Pygoplites diacanthus*)

    Rock Beauty (*Holacanthus tricolor*)

    Venusta (*Holacanthus venusta*)

Anthias (Subfamily Anthiinae): All

Batfishes: Pinnate or Redfinned (*Platax pinnatus*)

Butterflyfishes (Family Chaetodontidae): All

Filefishes: Longnosed (*Oxymonacanthus longirostris*)

Moorish Idol (*Zanclus cornutus*)

Parrotfishes (Family Scaridae): All

Ribbon Eel: Blue or Black (*Rhinomuraena quaesita*)

Seahorses and Pipefishes (Family Syngnathidae): All

Sweetlips: Clown (*Plectorhinchus chaetodontoides*)

Surgeonfishes/Tangs:

    Achilles (*Acanthurus achilles*)

    Lined (*Acanthurus lineatus*)

    Powderblue (*Acanthurus leucosternon*)

    Vlamingi's (*Naso vlamingii*)

    Whitecheek (*Acanthurus nigricans*)

Tilefishes (Family Malacanthidae): All

Wrasses:

    Cleaner (*Labroides* spp.)

    Leopard (*Macropharyngodon* spp.)

    Tamarin (*Anampses* spp.)

Neon Goby (*Gobiosoma oceanops*): small, attractive species that is easily bred in captivity and a good choice for quiet aquariums.

Wheeler's Watchman Goby (*Amblyeleotris wheeleri*): typical of many goby species that form associations with burrowing shrimp.

good choices. The larger gobies can be fed standard fare, although for some gobies like the shrimp, sleeper, or signal types, it is usually necessary to place some food near the bottom so that they can readily get to it. Most gobies should be kept only with other small, docile fishes.

Gobies feed on much of the fauna that tends to develop on and under live rock. The mandarinfishes (actually dragonets in the Family Callionymidae), in particular, require an established population of copepods and other small animals to be present on the live rock in order to survive. These fishes should not be added until an adequate population of such organisms has developed. Other groups that can easily starve are the previously mentioned sleeper and signal (or crab-eye) gobies, which actively sift the substrate for meaty foods. They demand special feeding or a very large expanse of well-populated live sand and are therefore not recommended for new aquarists.

Orbiculate Batfish (*Platax orbicularis*): docile but will outgrow smaller systems.

A much better group for beginners to choose from is that of the shrimp or watchman gobies (e.g., *Amblyeleotris* and *Cryptocentrus* spp.), which get their name from a fascinating symbiotic relationship they have with some types of snapping shrimps (*Alpheus* spp.). The goby lives in a burrow that has been excavated by the shrimp, who then forages near the entrance. When danger threatens, the goby alerts the nearly blind shrimp to retreat into the burrow. If a goby-shrimp pair can be purchased, their symbiotic behavior is sure to be entertaining.

Recommended species: Firefish (*Nemateleotris magnifica*); Purple Firefish (*Nemateleotris decora*); Neon Goby (*Gobiosoma oceanops*); Clown Goby (*Gobiodon citrinus*); and various members of the shrimp or watchman goby clan (e.g., *Amblyeleotris* and *Cryptocentrus* spp.).

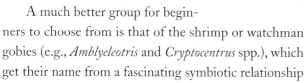

SELECTION TIP
Certain fishes (tangs and rabbitfishes, for example) are considered "ich magnets"— carriers of *Cryptocaryon irritans*. Use extra care when selecting, quarantining, and acclimating these fishes.

■ ■ ■

Family Ephippidae

NAMED FOR THEIR IMAGINED RESEMBLANCE to a bat (the flying mammal) when viewed from the side as they swim, the batfishes can make a dramatic display in a large, deep aquarium. Batfishes are generally hardy and do quite well as long as young, healthy specimens are obtained initially. (Older, larger batfishes do not always adapt well to captivity.)

The biggest problem with the batfishes is that they will outgrow most tanks in a very short time. These fishes are generally slow moving and docile and therefore will do best when housed with other docile specimens.

Recommended species: Orbiculate Batfish (*Platax orbicularis*); Teira Batfish (*Platax teira*).

Species to avoid: Pinnate or Red-finned Batfish (*Platax pinnatus*).

RABBITFISHES
Family Siganidae

LIKE THE SURGEONFISHES (discussed below), members of this family possess spines that they use for defensive purposes. However, the spines of the rabbitfishes are hollow and loaded with a venom that can inflict a painful sting. Fortunately, the rabbitfishes are nonaggressive herbivores that will actively graze on algal growths in the aquarium. Unlike many surgeonfishes, rabbitfishes can be housed in pairs or small groups.

Once acclimated, rabbitfishes are quite hardy, but must be offered plenty of green material in their diet and should always be handled with care to avoid accidental stings.

Recommended species: Foxface (*Siganus vulpinus*); Onespot Rabbitfish (*Siganus unimaculatus*); Magnificent Rabbitfish (*Siganus magnificus*).

SURGEONFISHES (TANGS)
Family Acanthuridae

THE SURGEONFISH FAMILY contains some of the most popular fishes kept in marine tanks. They have earned their "surgeon" name because of the sharp spine at the base of their tail that resembles a surgeon's scalpel. This spine is nonvenomous but is to be avoided—a large tang can inflict a deep cut.

A surgeonfish should be offered a diet high in vegetable matter, such as *Spirulina* algae, nori, romaine lettuce, or spinach, as well as an occasional treat of fresh *Caulerpa* algae. These fishes should be fed several times daily as they have a high metabolism.

The biggest drawback in keeping surgeonfishes is that they are very vulnerable to parasites, particularly immediately after shipping and introduction to a cap-tive system. Unless adequately quarantined, they pose a high risk of infecting other fishes in the tank. Most tangs grow quite large, so adults should be housed in a tank of not less than 70 to 90 gallons. Unless the system is very large, keeping only one tang per species (or genus) will prevent constant and often terminal turf wars.

Recommended species: Yellow Tang (*Zebrasoma flavescens*); Yellowtail Blue or Hippo Tang (*Paracanthurus hepatus*); Purple Tang (*Zebrasoma xanthurum*).

TRIGGERFISHES
Family Balistidae

JUDGED ON A COMBINATION of bold color and outgoing behavior patterns, it would be hard to find a group of fishes more interesting than the triggers. Exceptionally graceful swimmers, they can lock themselves into tight,

Onespot Rabbitfish (*Siganus unimaculatus*): one of a number of rabbitfishes that are good herbivores and can be kept in groups.

Magnificent Rabbitfish (*Siganus magnificus*): a less common species; its venomous spines are typical of the rabbitfish group.

Purple Tang (*Zebrasoma xanthurum*): a prized and somewhat pricey Red Sea species that feeds heavily on vegetable matter.

Yellow Tang (*Zebrasoma flavescens*): adding a blaze of color, this is a territorial species best kept singly in all but very large tanks.

Redtooth or Niger Triggerfish (*Odonus niger*): one of the triggerfishes that is less likely to attack its tankmates.

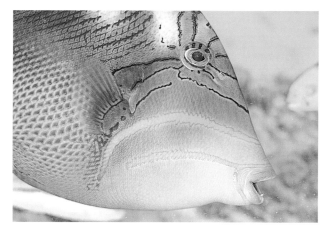

Queen Triggerfish (*Balistes vetula*): with a nasty bite and a hostile disposition, this is a fish for aggressive collections only.

rocky places by erecting their stout dorsal spine, and can blow prey items, such as sea urchins, over onto their backs in preparation for attacking their vulnerable undersides. Triggers are rugged and easy to keep, but their unpredictable or aggressive nature and their tendency to pick on or attack virtually any and all of their tankmates precludes most of them from being considered good community fishes. Some triggers will live for years without causing problems, while others suddenly decide to eat or maim anything that moves in their tank. To be safe, choose among the less aggressive species and keep a triggerfish with other large species that are able to fend for themselves (lionfishes, morays, big wrasses, and the like). Also note that a large triggerfish can inflict significant damage on an unsuspecting aquarist who nonchalantly places his or her hand in the tank.

Less aggressive species: Redtooth or Niger Trigger (*Odonus niger*); Bluethroated Trigger (*Xanthichthys auromarginatus*); Picasso Trigger (*Rhinecanthus aculeatus*).

More aggressive species: Orangelined or Undulated Trigger (*Balistapus undulatus*); Queen Trigger (*Balistes vetula*); Clown Trigger (*Balistoides conspicillum*).

PUFFERS & PORCUPINEFISHES
Families Tetraodontidae & Diodontidae

NEW AQUARISTS are often drawn to the puffers, which can have big eyes and endearing personalities—begging for food and forming attachments to their keepers. While hardy and easy to maintain, the large puffers and porcupinefishes are notorious for nipping—or eating—other fishes and invertebrates. For this reason, none of the species of puffers or porcupinefishes can be safely recommended for a smaller, less aggressive community tank. Some of the puffers grow to more than a foot in length and require aquariums in the 100-to-200-gallon range.

The small pufferfishes known as tobies (or sharpnose puffers) are a better choice for many hobbyists. Members of the genus *Canthigaster*, these often-colorful fishes are every bit as personable as their larger relatives. Some tobies have a reputation as fin nippers, but they are generally docile and do best in a less aggressive setting.

Recommended species: various tobies (*Canthigaster* spp.), also known as sharpnose puffers, including the Sharpnose Puffer (*Canthigaster rostrata*); the Saddled or Valentini Toby (*Canthigaster valentini*); and the Hawaiian or Whitespotted Toby (*Canthigaster jactator*).

Saddled or Valentini Toby (*Canthigaster valentini*): one of the smaller puffers that can make for an interesting aquatic pet.

INVERTEBRATES

SINCE THE DISPLAY TANK will not be treated with copper or any medications, it will be possible to keep some invertebrates in addition to the fishes. These animals will not only add interesting behaviors, but many will also help keep the aquarium clean.

Snails and urchins will graze algae from the live rock and glass. Brittle stars and small hermit crabs will eat detritus and keep the substrate stirred up. Certain species of shrimp will aid in disease reduction by acting as cleaners, removing parasites from infected fish.

Most of the invertebrates listed in the chart above require no special care and do not even need to be fed directly. They do need to be acclimated to the tank water over a period of at least 30 minutes and given adequate places to hide. They will do quite well and perform their cleaning services constantly as long as no medications are added.

SELECTING HEALTHY FISHES

ONCE YOU'VE NARROWED the choice of specific fishes for the tank, it is time—at last—to begin purchasing them. For a novice, it can be rather difficult to determine if a particular fish in a dealer's tank is healthy or not, but with a little practice and an understanding of what to look for, it becomes easier. (This is a learned art, something acquired by watching and keeping fishes.) At this point, it helps to have at least a mental listing of the species that you plan to place in your aquarium. Try to have alternatives, and be prepared to special-order some fishes—it is unlikely that even the best-stocked shop will have all of your first choices immediately on hand. I urge you to be patient and select the species you really want, looking for specimens that are healthy and eating.

Starting with healthy fishes will greatly increase your chances of having them survive during the crucial first few weeks after purchase. This is the period when many fishes have the greatest risk of dying prematurely. Once they get through this initial 4-to-6-week period, the chances of their living a long life in a home tank are very good. Early deaths can be caused by any number of factors, including the stress of capture and shipping, the inability to acclimate to captive conditions or accept food, the stress of being introduced to a new tank containing aggressive tankmates, or disease.

The first and simplest rule is that the fish must be

STOPPING CYANIDE
Watching for Signs of Poisoned Fishes

One benefit of more aquarists buying only fishes that have been in the dealer's tanks for several days and that are eating well is that the chances of buying fishes that have been collected with cyanide are greatly reduced.

In many areas of the Philippines and in parts of Indonesia, collectors of live fishes for Asian food markets and the aquarium trade use sodium cyanide to stun and remove fishes from the reef. Cyanide kills many fishes on the spot, along with the live coral colonies in which they were hiding, and usually leaves the stunned survivors with poor prospects for long-term survival.

Cyanide has been implicated in damaging both the nervous and digestive systems of fishes, and cyanided specimens may either refuse to eat or may eat greedily but still waste away. By asking to see a fish eat, the aquarium keeper is applying a simple test that can help screen out possible victims of cyanide poisoning. Be extremely wary of any fish that looks dazed and/or completely uninterested in food. Also watch for the fish

that eats but appears emaciated. (Obviously, there are many reasons that a fish might refuse to eat, and ignoring food is far from proof that a specimen has been caught with cyanide. However, any fish that steadfastly shuns food is a very poor aquarium prospect.)

While there is no sure-fire way to test if a fish that has reached the retail market was caught with cyanide, many international organizations are attempting to curb the use of cyanide in collecting fishes in the source countries. Marine aquarium fishes certified as "net caught," "cyanide-free," or "sustainably harvested" may be available in the near future.

When more aquarists refuse to buy suspect livestock, we will see improvements in the overall quality of marine life offered for sale. More important, we can help prevent coral reefs from being decimated by cyanide. The use of nets and traps can give native collectors a profitable way to catch fishes without harming live coral heads. This, in turn, will help ensure a healthy, sustainable harvest from their reefs.

---

swimming normally. That is, it should present itself well and look robust as it moves around the tank. The fish shouldn't appear to be struggling when it swims, but should glide effortlessly through the water or move in the characteristic manner of its species. (Some fishes have odd or distinctive swimming methods, which you will quickly come to recognize.)

Avoid any fish that is gasping at the surface or constantly hovering with its nose in a corner. A fish of a species that normally swims in the open should not be spending all of its time hiding. Many fishes will hide immediately after arrival in any new environment, so ask how long the fish has been in the tank. Also, many fishes, such as groupers, grammas, and eels, naturally spend much of their time in hiding; it helps to learn the characteristics of a family to know what is or isn't abnormal behavior.

One other swimming behavior should also be noted as a warning sign. Occasionally you will see stereotypical actions in which a fish constantly repeats the same pattern of behavior. Typical examples include a fish constantly swimming in a circular pattern around a coral head or around the same spot in a tank, or doing endless laps, back and forth the length of the tank. The fish does not stop to forage and swims intently without varying the route—acting oblivious to its surroundings. These signs can be indicative of something amiss physically or psychologically with the specimen. Often these fishes will not adapt well to captivity.

In addition to normal swimming behavior, a number of other characteristics should be examined before purchasing a fish. If a normal swimming pattern is frequently disrupted by the fish scratching or rubbing against objects in the tank or shaking itself, there may be parasites present or other health problems developing. The fish's eyes should be clear and without marks. The eyes should also be flush to the body with no indication of swelling. Bulging eyes can indicate a serious and difficult-to-treat fungal or bacterial infection.

The fish should not have any marks or lesions on its body nor should it have any growths that take away from the sleekness of its body. Do not buy any specimen with such symptoms. If the fish is unusual and especially desirable, ask the shop if they will hold it for you until it is cured of the problem.

Torn or slightly ripped fins should not necessarily disqualify a fish from being purchased. If they are only slightly frayed, fins on an otherwise healthy specimen will heal up very quickly in a clean tank. On the other hand, badly shredded or missing fins, or any growths on the fins, can be signs of serious problems.

Very few dealers will intentionally sell a fish that is exhibiting any of these easy-to-spot symptoms. (Inexperienced or harried staff may miss them, however, and you should personally screen each fish you buy.) Another subtle sign to watch for is the fish's breathing, which should not be labored or rapid—nor should the gills open widely during respiration. This is usually a sign of severe stress, and the fish may not have long to live or may be fighting an infection that has attacked its gills.

Another warning sign is abnormal coloration, either excessively dark or very light at an inappropriate time. A fish may show these abnormal coloring patterns when stressed. Some observers believe that fishes may also display unusually intense colors when suffering the after-effects of being caught with cyanide. However, in a group of normal-looking fish of the same species, the brightest-colored one may just be dominant, and vibrant coloration can also be a sign of vigor and strength.

Quick Test

THE BEST INDICATION that a fish is healthy is that it eats with gusto when fed. Refusing food can be a sign of many different problems, including advancing disease, possibly collection by cyanide, and prolonged stress and star-

vation during collection and shipment. Before purchasing any fish, you should ask to see it fed in the dealer's tank.

Hardy, easy-to-keep fishes will usually accept flake food without hesitation. (Assuming they haven't recently had a heavy meal.) For more expensive specimens, I like to see them offered several types of food. If flake food doesn't work, thawed frozen food can be tried, followed by live food, such as adult brine shrimp.

Besides demonstrating whether the fish is healthy, the watch-them-eat test should also show that the fish is not limited to eating only a single item. By seeing the fish offered a selection of foods, it can also be determined what the fish prefers. If it eats only one type of food (virtually all healthy fish will find live food impossible to resist), it may be difficult to wean onto other foods and may become malnourished.

If a fish doesn't eat on one occasion, ask the dealer if he or she will hold it so that on a return trip in a couple of days an attempt at feeding it again can be observed. On this visit, a different assortment of foods may be tried. This will increase the odds that something will be found that the fish will eat.

One other thing to look for when seeing if a fish eats in a dealer's tank is how it interacts with the other fishes feeding in the same tank. That is, do its tankmates outcompete it for food or does it dominate all of the other fishes in the tank and prevent them from feeding? These behavior patterns can be indicative of how a fish might interact with others in your system.

Another measure of a fish's eating habits is its physical condition. A severely shrunken or pinched belly may be a bad sign, and the fish's head should not have a narrowing, thinness, or concave area behind the eyes. This shrinking is indicative of poor nutrition or starvation and means that the fish has lost weight. This is often a result of the fish being stressed or having come through a long period of shipping and holding without food. It may not be able to tolerate additional stress, and should be considered a poor prospect.

SELECTION TIP
When buying a new fish, always ask to see it fed in the dealer's tank. Never bring home a fish that refuses all foods.

■ ■ ■

As a general rule, if a fish doesn't eat in the dealer's tank, don't buy it. Considerable expense can be saved by simply following this guideline. Many aquarists feel that the care they will provide will be superior to that of any retail shop, that they will offer more varied foods, and that they will be able to get the fish to eat. In my experience, this is the exception, rather than the rule. Only in rare instances will a nonfeeding fish start to eat when placed in a home tank. Remember, some may have been severely damaged by cyanide collection or heavy stress before they ever arrive in your local shop, and these specimens have very poor chances of survival. In general, more fish will die than will be saved if purchased when they are refusing food.

ACCLIMATING NEW SPECIMENS

ONCE A HEALTHY FISH has been purchased and brought home, the next step is to acclimate it properly. Many hardy marine fishes will settle into a new aquarium with no problem, but getting some new fishes to survive in a tank—particularly a new tank—is sometimes difficult.

The first month appears to be the period when fish losses are at their peak. I have learned the hard way that unless care is taken to introduce fishes properly mortali-

ties in the first weeks after they are acquired can be very high—approaching 50% at times. At first I thought that such mortalities in my own tanks were due to poor water quality or some other factor. However when I compared my own experiences with corals, which live in the same water and were acclimated in the same way, the picture was significantly different. The survival rate of the corals was over 80%. I knew that some other factors must be responsible for early mortality of new fishes.

Other than water quality, part of the losses are simply due to the process of adding fishes to a closed system. Unlike a coral reef, an aquarium is a very small aquatic environment. In moving a specimen from the ocean to a relatively tiny tank, several factors come into play.

For one, the territory of the fish is greatly reduced, which can produce significant consequences. As an example, some damselfishes have territories in their natural habitat of about 6 square feet per specimen. In all but the largest tanks, one of these damsels will take over a territory as big as the entire tank. Therefore, if any similar damsels or competing species are introduced once this fish has established its turf, they will be attacked as intruders just as they would be in nature. The limited area of the aquarium makes it difficult or impossible for the new fishes to avoid the aggressive individual. This badgering may result in the new fishes being unable to eat.

In order for any aquarium fish to acclimate successfully, it must be able to overcome three important factors when placed in a new tank:

• Stress from capture and shipping;
• Adjustment to new surroundings, water, and food;
• Aggression from current tank residents.

The first difficulty may be reduced by allowing the fish to remain in the dealer's tank for a week or so to get accustomed to captivity—provided the store's policy includes holding specimens for its customers. For a small deposit, some dealers will allow a fish to be put on hold. This time period will allow it to settle down as well as to manifest any hidden ailments. (If the fish becomes ill or dies while in the dealer's short-term care, the deposit will usually be applied to a replacement purchase. Ask about the policy in place at the stores where you shop.)

After this initial period, the fish can be purchased

TEN COMMON STOCKING MISTAKES

1. Overstocking.
2. Not quarantining new fishes.
3. Adding a new fish without adequate social acclimation.
4. Mismatching fishes of different temperaments.
5. Assuming that all large fishes are aggressive and all small fishes are docile.
6. Buying large, mature specimens, rather than starting with juveniles or small adults.
7. Not allowing space for the fishes' growth.
8. Buying "bargain" fishes by price, rather than from sources that have the healthiest, most robust specimens.
9. Adding aggressive species first.
10. Constantly adding "one more fish" to the tank.

and brought home, but not placed directly into the display tank. Any new fish must first be placed in a quarantine tank where it can start its adjustment. In the quarantine tank, a new acquisition can be pampered and medicated, if necessary, to build its strength and to acclimate it to the water and foods you will provide.

The aquarist's first job, then, is to deal with any differences in water chemistry between the store water and the quarantine tank's water. The simplest method is this:

• Place the shipping bag containing the new specimen into a small bucket, plastic tub, or other waterproof container that will hold the bag in an upright position.

• Open the top of the bag and remove one-quarter to one-third of the shipping water. Replace this with a like amount of water from the quarantine tank. Repeat this procedure every 10 to 15 minutes for 30 to 45 minutes; by the end, the bag water temperature and chemistry will be essentially the same as those of the water in the quarantine tank where the fish is to be placed.

• Pour the water through a net, catching the fish and allowing the water to run down a drain or into the bucket. Immediately release the fish into the quarantine tank. Alternatively, carefully pour off all the water from the bag, being sure that the fish doesn't escape, then quickly slip the specimen from the shipping bag into the quarantine tank. (If you have previously been a freshwater hobbyist, you may have to unlearn the habit of floating the shipping bag for 15 minutes in your display tank and then dumping both water and fish into the aquarium. This is a poor procedure, even for freshwater fishes.)

• Be sure the lights are dimmed in the quarantine tank, but don't put a new fish into total darkness—this can be just as stressful and disorienting as placing it abruptly under bright aquarium lights. If the room is dark, leave a dim light or nightlight on.

> ### ACCLIMATION TIP
> After a prolonged period in a closed plastic bag, shipping water will be high in ammonium and low in oxygen with a low pH. Never acclimate in the bag by adding an airstone. This can rapidly elevate the pH, causing ammonium to convert to more toxic ammonia. A better method is to remove a portion of the bag water and replace it with water from the system where the fish will be placed. Repeat every 10 to 15 minutes over a period of 30 to 45 minutes.
>
> ■ ■ ■

THE QUARANTINE PROCESS

IN AQUARIUM INHABITANTS, as in humans, preventing disease is far easier than treating it. For this reason, the establishment of a quarantine tank separate from the main display tank is a very worthwhile investment. A quarantine tank allows a fish to become acclimated not only to its new surroundings, but also to just being in a captive environment. The period after capture and shipping is a time when the fish is highly vulnerable to infectious disease or the attack of parasites. A quarantine tank allows these problems to be treated early, and away from the main tank. This lessens the likelihood that parasites will be spread within the close confines of the main aquarium.

The quarantine tank need not be anything elaborate. A 10-to-20-gallon tank with a sponge filter, cover, heater, and some inert hiding places (plastic flowerpots or PVC plumbing fittings or pieces of pipe) are all that are really necessary. Since this tank will never have the heavy biological load of a full display aquarium, the bacterial filter does not need to be as large as that of the main tank.

The establishment of beneficial bacteria in the sponge filter is quite simple. After saltwater is mixed up to the desired salinity, the sponge filter is installed in the quarantine tank. After this has been allowed to run for a couple of days, a small piece of uncured live rock can be added to the tank. The bacteria on the rock will then colonize the sponge, and the dead material on the rock will act as an ammonia source. In this way, after approximately 3 to 4 weeks, an active biological filter will be established. An alternative is to place the sponge in an established tank for a week or so and allow it to become colonized. Yet another method is to take some gravel from an established tank and place it around the sponge to act as a source of bacteria. In place of live rock, a mesh bag of sand from a healthy, established tank can be added, along with some pieces of food that are allowed to decompose in the tank to act as an ammonia source. (Once the sponge filter is colonized by bacteria, the live rock and sand can be removed.)

After the bacteria have become established, as evidenced by zero readings from ammonia and nitrite tests, the tank can be used to quarantine new or sick fishes. Again, any fishes to be placed in quarantine should first be acclimated to the water in the tank.

As an extra precaution, some aquarists give new arrivals a freshwater or medicated dip to reduce their parasite load before quarantine. A dip is usually not a cure per se, but it does lower the parasite load to such a degree that the disease is usually easier to manage than if the fishes had not been dipped. Experts are strongly divided about new hobbyists giving dips, with some arguing that they work well and others advising that they are stressful to the specimens. If in doubt, skip the dipping procedure and rely on the quarantine period and your own careful observations to stop any problems.

Every new fish, whether given a dip treatment or not, should be placed in the quarantine tank for 3 to 4 weeks. During this time, it should be fed one or more times daily and carefully observed for any signs of disease. If symptoms appear, they should be treated according to the methods outlined in the disease section (beginning on page 133). The fish should show no signs of disease for the last 2 weeks of its quarantine period before being allowed into the display aquarium. During this time, if any new fishes are introduced to the quarantine tank, the clock must start all over again. Remember that a new specimen can be carrying pathogens, and it can infect the fishes already in quarantine.

Equipment can also be a source of contamination. It is good practice to have nets, a thermometer, and any other movable equipment dedicated to the quarantine tank to avoid contamination of the display tank. In addition, the quarantine system should be emptied and disinfected with a chlorine bleach solution between uses, especially if any diseases were treated in the tank. (Sterilize the filter sponge and return it to the display system to become re-inoculated with bacteria.)

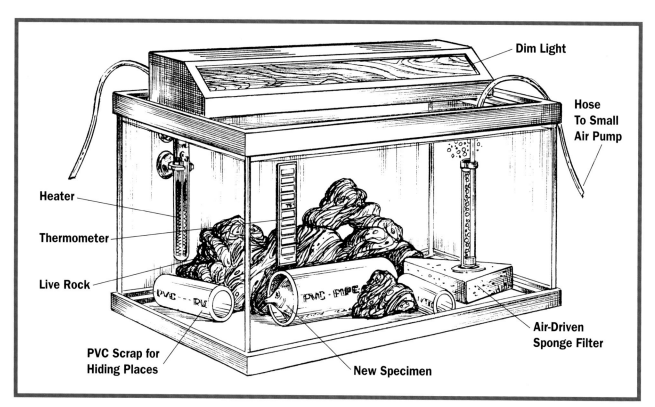

A basic quarantine system is simple and inexpensive to set up and will repay the aquarist repeatedly by preventing contagious disease outbreaks in the display aquarium. By quarantining all new arrivals for 3 to 4 weeks, the hobbyist will avoid many unnecessary losses.

Again, this quarantine/acclimation phase is crucial because a large percentage of preventable fish deaths occur in the first month. With some simple procedures and planning, these losses can be reduced dramatically.

LOW-SALINITY QUARANTINE

AN OLD TRICK OF THE FISH TRADE has recently begun to attract the attention of amateur aquarists. By keeping the salinity of the quarantine system significantly lower than that of natural seawater, many fishkeepers have noted dramatic improvement in survival rates and elimination of such common parasitic diseases as *Cryptocaryon irritans* (marine ich), *Amyloodinium ocellatum* (marine velvet), and several types of problem worms. As pointed out previously, the parasites have a much lower tolerance for decreased salinity than do the fishes, which can adapt to a wide range of salinity conditions.

As radical as it sounds, the specific gravity of the quarantine tank may be lowered to the level of 1.010 to 1.012 (about 15 ppt salinity), and most fishes will acclimate readily. Some experts simply keep their quarantine tanks at this level as a standard procedure. (Nonbony fishes, such as sharks and rays, along with many invertebrates, will not tolerate these low-salinity conditions.) A typical 3-to-4-week quarantine in low-salinity water is an effective method of eliminating parasites without the use of possibly harmful drugs.

INTRODUCTION TO THE DISPLAY TANK

ONCE A FISH HAS BEEN ACCLIMATED and has successfully gone through the quarantine procedure, it needs to be carefully introduced to its new tankmates. Because the water conditions in the quarantine tank and your display aquarium won't be identical, the fish should be caught, placed in a small bucket with quarantine tank water, and run through the acclimation procedure explained on page 112, gradually removing and replacing

> "AS RADICAL AS IT SOUNDS, THE SPECIFIC GRAVITY OF THE QUARANTINE TANK MAY BE LOWERED TO THE LEVEL OF 1.010 TO 1.012 AND MOST FISHES WILL ACCLIMATE READILY."
>
> ■ ■ ■

small quantities of the transfer water over a period of 30 to 45 minutes.

If you anticipate aggression problems between the new specimen and your existing community of fishes, the newcomer may have to be introduced gradually. In this case, a covered holding container is placed in the display tank and the fish is placed in it. A 1-to-2-gallon clear specimen container that can be attached to the side of the tank works well for this purpose, or a large filter box or nursery tank can be refitted. Numerous holes should be drilled in the bottom and sides so that the tank's water can circulate freely into and out of the box. In addition, the output from a powerhead should be directed toward the container so that there will be a constant flow of water. A piece of PVC pipe like that used in the quarantine tank should be placed in the box to provide a hiding area to help the fish feel secure in its new environment.

This clear container will allow the new fish to view its surroundings and tankmates from a protected position, while at the same time permitting the tank's residents to view the newcomer. Any fish with aggressive tendencies will now display them by charging at the box. At first the new fish will cower when approached, but the box will prevent any injury, and over time (usually several days), the frequency and intensity of these attacks will diminish. The newcomer should be kept in the protective container until no attacks occur. Usually this takes anywhere from 2 to 10 days. Occasionally, it will take longer.

If aggression does not subside after 2 weeks, it may be necessary to remove the aggressive individual and place *it* in the box, then release the new fish into the tank. This step may be necessary because the tank's older residents have established territories and know all of the tank's hiding places. If a new fish is introduced among these aggressive fishes with clearly staked-out territories, the newcomer will be at a distinct disadvantage. It may be killed outright or harassed to such an extent that it never eats and eventually dies.

Several things can be done to reduce this aggression once the tank's older residents are re-released into the tank. The live rock or other aquascaping materials can be rearranged in order to force the old fishes to establish new territories. In addition, if several new fishes are added simultaneously before the aggressive fish is returned to the tank, the actions of the aggressive fish will be spread out, or diffused, thus minimizing their impact on any one fish.

ONE-PER-FAMILY RULE

MANY FISHES ON THE REEF have evolved territorial behaviors that are directed against their own kind or against other fishes that pose a threat to their food supply. A well-known example is the surgeonfishes or tangs, which are notorious for fighting when confined in smaller aquariums. This aggression is directed at members of their own species as well as other species of tangs in the same genus, and even fishes that are similar in coloration or shape.

Other commonly available aquarium groups that display strong territorial instincts are the damselfishes (including some of the clownfishes), the angelfishes, and some of the basses and basslike fishes, such as the dottybacks and anthias. In smaller tanks, it is often advisable to include no more than one member of a particular family. Two tangs or two angelfishes—whether of the same species or not—will often fight until one eventually weakens and dies. In larger systems with plenty of live rock and places to seek shelter, the rules can change somewhat, but aggression between fishes can never be taken lightly.

For example, I've seen a Resplendent Angelfish (*Centropyge resplendens*) attack a Starck's Damselfish (*Abudefduf starcki*) that had similar coloration; I had a Springer's Dottyback (*Pseudochromis springeri*) kill a Six-line Wrasse (*Pseudocheilinus hexataenia*) with a similar body shape; and I had a Powderblue Tang (*Acanthurus*

leucosternon) harass a Red Sea Sailfin Tang (*Zebrasoma desjardinii*) into starvation by not allowing it to graze in peace. Two butterflyfishes of the same or similar-looking species will also compete with each other, sometimes in subtle ways not immediately recognized by the new aquarist. The dominant fish tends to get the food, constantly outmaneuvering the other until it starves.

When introducing a fish to a tank that already has a member of that same family or species, special precautions should be taken. Groups of three or more fishes often do better than (nonmated) "pairs," with more chances to diffuse the aggression.

Neither I, nor any other hobbyist I know, claims to be a complete master at mixing marine species. In the first place, there are too many new and strange fishes to learn about. Beyond that, placing specimens together is more art than science, and one never quite knows for sure what the outcome will be.

For the beginner, the best route is to select among the many tried-and-true hardy and less aggressive species listed in this chapter. Avoid placing two members of the same species or family in the same modest-sized tank, unless they are naturally docile or paired-off. (In very small tanks, even docile species may tend to fight.) Don't buy hard-to-keep species until your skills have grown and your system is well established.

While the suggestions in this chapter require more time and patience than just bringing home any fish that catches your eye and dumping it directly into the display tank, they can greatly reduce your losses of new fishes. Losing specimens can quickly drive beginning hobbyists to drain their tanks and give up. If your first specimens thrive, this success will help build the confidence to try new and more challenging species.

Banggai Cardinalfish (*Pterapogon kauderni*): a mouthbrooding marine species that will reproduce in proper aquarium settings.

> "FOR THE BEGINNER, THE BEST ROUTE IS TO SELECT AMONG THE MANY TRIED-AND-TRUE HARDY AND LESS AGGRESSIVE SPECIES LISTED IN THIS CHAPTER. . . . DON'T BUY HARD-TO-KEEP SPECIES UNTIL YOUR SKILLS HAVE GROWN AND YOUR SYSTEM IS WELL ESTABLISHED."
>
> ■ ■ ■

CHAPTER 6

FEEDING & MAINTENANCE

*Simple Routines for Keeping Fishes Well Fed
and the System Attractive*

PERHAPS THE MOST URGENT CONCERN of new aquarium owners is feeding their fishes, while their last priority is the on-going maintenance of their water quality. In truth, the feeding of hardy marine fishes is not particularly difficult, but the neglect of routine caretaking chores can quickly lead to a tank that first loses its beauty and then its livestock. Smart feeding and minimal maintenance, however, do go hand-in-hand. Overfeeding—easily the most common mistake of home aquarists—will demand more time spent coping with wastes and all their unpleasant consequences. The aquarist with a heavy feeding hand will find that water quality declines more rapidly, filters need more attention, and growth of nuisance algae speeds up.

Left: evening mealtime in a 700-gallon home aquarium. **Above:** hand-feeding a Scarlet Cleaner Shrimp (*Lysmata debelius*).

Fortunately, the stability of your filtration system and the selection of easy-to-feed first fishes is designed to provide the newcomer with a reasonable degree of leeway. Good feeding skills and maintenance routines take some time to develop, but there is nothing particularly difficult or burdensome about any of the day-to-day chores done to keep a system running.

FEEDING BASICS

MANY FISHKEEPERS take particular joy in feeding their animals and observing their eating behaviors. This can be a simple task, as a well-acclimated and carefully chosen marine fish should eat voraciously. Resisting the temptation to feed your fishes whenever they act hungry, however, may be the hardest lesson to learn.

Many marine fishes are in a constant search for food when on the reef, and some graze or nibble throughout the day. In fact, much of a fish's energy is expended either searching for food or trying not to become a meal for something else. Many species of reef fishes search for food and eat throughout their active hours. (Some larger predators, such as moray eels and groupers, feed less frequently.) As a result, the practice of dumping a large quantity of food into the tank once a day is not particularly conducive to the fishes' long-term health. Not only do they tend to gorge themselves during this feeding, but because most hobbyists tend to overdo this binge meal, some food will remain uneaten, adding to the nitrogenous waste load that your filtration system must handle.

A much better method of feeding the tank—and realistically it is the tank that is being fed—is to provide a number of smaller feedings over the course of the day. When I feed, I try to give no more than the fishes can consume within 1 to 2 minutes. (The old rule of giving the fishes 10 minutes to clean everything up seems to encourage many fishkeepers to shovel in enough food to last the full 10 minutes. This almost guarantees that uneaten food will find its way into the substrate, drift into nooks in the aquascaping, and be left to decay in the tank or filtration system.)

Many of the hardy species of marine fishes can be maintained on a properly sized single meal per day, especially with live rock to provide grazing and foraging opportunities. However, two feedings per day is much better, perhaps one quick feeding with a high quality flake food and one meal from the freezer. (Frozen marine foods are a mainstay for most serious fishkeepers.)

With a number of very active and challenging-to-keep species in my tanks, I have developed the habit of giving four meals each day. This may seem like a difficult schedule to maintain, but with a little planning it can be made quite simple. A suggested schedule starts with a light feeding in the morning, before the aquarist leaves the house. The tank lights may not yet be on, but there is usually sufficient ambient light in the room for many of the fishes to be active. A light feeding will satisfy these active individuals. The second feeding is given right af-

> **"THERE IS NOTHING PARTICULARLY DIFFICULT OR BURDENSOME ABOUT ANY OF THE DAY-TO-DAY CHORES DONE TO KEEP A SYSTEM RUNNING."**
>
> ■ ■ ■

ter coming home at the end of the day. This will be the heaviest feeding, as the lights should be on and all of the fishes should be active at this time. The third feeding is provided a couple of hours later in midevening, and a final feeding is given at least a half hour before the lights are turned off. Having the lights remain on for a time after the last feeding reduces the likelihood that any food will be missed and fall to the bottom where it will decompose. These feeding times come at approximately 8 A.M., 6 P.M., 8 P.M., and 10 P.M.

If this feeding regimen simply won't work for you, the easy solution is to use an automatic feeder with a timer. Several reliable and affordable units (either plug-in or battery-powered) are available and will deliver a relatively constant serving of flakes or other dry food at designated times each day.

Whatever your schedule, the fishes should never be overfed, and a single feeding should not leave them stuffed with food and displaying grossly protruding abdomens. If this occurs occasionally it should do no harm, but fish routinely allowed to gorge themselves have been found to die prematurely with fatty livers. (This cause of death is also thought to be a possible consequence of inadequate exercise due to poor water movement. In order to reduce the likelihood of your fishes developing this problem, keep the feeding of overly fatty foods to a minimum and provide strong water flow within the tank.)

If the fishes are to go unfed for a couple of days, they should not be overfed beforehand. Not only does this not keep them full for the duration, but the unusual feast will inevitably be followed by an increase in waste production. If your fishes have been consistently well fed, going a few days without food should not harm them. Also the algae and life on the live rock will help to sustain them for several days. (Many fishes routinely survive up to 2 weeks without being fed between being the time of collection and their arrival in the dealer's tanks.)

Starvation should not be a problem with most of the more common, popular marine species. However, chronic underfeeding will result in the fishes getting gradually thinner, particularly in the area behind their eyes.

Lastly, the tank should not be fed every time the keeper passes by and the fishes follow along "looking hungry." This behavior does not indicate hunger as much as it shows that the fishes have trained the owner to respond to their "begging." Overfed fishes get unnaturally bulky, their natural behavior patterns rarely show, and they often suffer shortened lifespans. I like to feed my fishes at different spots along the tank and on a schedule, rather than every time they act hungry. In the long run, both the fishes and the water quality will benefit.

ESSENTIAL VARIETY

In nature, most fishes eat a varied diet, and this should also be the case in the home aquarium. A constant diet of one type of flake, frozen, or freeze-dried food will simply not keep marine fishes healthy and vibrant over the long term. Many successful aquarists offer a daily meal of (thawed) frozen food, with one or two small offerings of high-quality dried or flake foods and occasional treats of fresh seafood or vegetable matter. A varied diet produces positive consequences in a number of ways. Frozen foods provide the palatability and closest approximation to natural prey items and are a mainstay of many diets. Dried and flake foods allow quick, small feedings without going to the freezer. Variety helps a fish maintain not only its vitality, but also its color.

Besides the ubiquitous flake foods, the choices of appropriate items are numerous. Over the last few years, a large number of frozen marine foods have come onto the market, including krill, plankton, brine shrimp, silversides, squid, sea urchin, and marine sponges—as well as blended diets—some of them designed for specific types of fish. Some freshwater items, such as bloodworms, glassworms, daphnia, *Mysis* shrimp, and mosquito larvae can be offered to marine fishes. In addition, fresh or frozen items from the fish market, such as shrimp, fish fillets, and clams or oysters on the half shell can be given as occasional treats.

The delivery of these foods is rather simple. In the case of the solid items, such as plankton or krill, a piece of food of the desired size should be cut from the frozen block. This piece should then be allowed to thaw before feeding. To reduce the introduction of inedible nutrients (juices and very fine particulate matter), the food can be placed in a fine mesh net, like those used for brine shrimp, then briefly rinsed under running water. (In reef aquariums, this protein-rich juice may be consumed by corals and filter-feeders, but for most fish-only tanks, such liquefied waste should be kept out.)

Care should be taken to wash any fresh foods from the fish market before adding them to the tank. I would recommend buying from a market that has a reputation for selling good, fresh fish. This is particularly important in the case of shrimp, which may be chemically treated to retain a false appearance of freshness. (A sniff test will reveal shrimp that has been hit with chlorine to disguise its true condition.) If fresh clams or oysters are offered, their shells should be thoroughly scrubbed under freshwater not only to remove any dirt or silt, but also to help remove any bacteria that may be present.

Frozen, blended fish foods bought in cubes or thin sheets should be lightly thawed before being gently broken up and added to the tank. Do not allow the foods to

Recommended foods for saltwater fishes include, from left to right, high-quality marine dry flakes, frozen foods of many types, and freeze-dried items, such as enriched krill.

FEEDING TIPS

1. If a new fish completely refuses to eat, it may be necessary to feed it through the water. This can be done because saltwater fishes are constantly consuming water. Fructose, glucose, or dextrose (corn syrup) can be added at the rate of 1 teaspoon per 5 or 10 gallons of quarantine water. This is, however, only a short-term solution. Do *not* use sucrose (common table sugar).

2. Don't worry if a fish does not eat for the first day or two after being acquired. However, if a week passes without the fish eating, drastic measures may need to be taken (see suggestion #5).

3. If you don't want your fishes to gather in one spot every time someone passes the tank, vary the location where the food is added.

4. Be sure that all food is cleaned up completely within 1 to 2 minutes of its being added to the tank. Reduce the amount if it takes your fishes longer than that to consume the offering.

5. Irresistible foods that can sometimes initiate a feeding response in a new specimen include: live adult brine shrimp, a fresh clam (on the half-shell) from the seafood market, or live freshwater items (worms, grass shrimp, etc.). Try a variety of tempting items if the first doesn't appeal to the fish.

6. If a fish begins to show signs of head and lateral line erosion (HLLE), it should be treated early by increasing the offerings of vegetable-based foods— frozen marine algae ration, *Spirulina*, nori, leaf lettuce, or vitamin-soaked flake foods.

---

thaw too long or they will become entirely liquid. If the food reaches this point, it should not be added to the tank, as it will only contribute to the waste load.

Most of the foods discussed so far have been primarily of animal origin. Just about all fishes, however, should receive some food of vegetable origin. This is important, as improper diet has been implicated in the development of disfiguring head and lateral line erosion (HLLE, also called hole-in-the-head). Also, the coloration of many marine fishes can only be maintained if a proper diet containing vegetable matter is provided.

In the wild, many marine fishes get their vegetable matter by grazing on algae that grow on the reef. Due to the limited size of most aquariums and the type of algae that typically grow in closed systems, not enough algae of the proper type will be present in most tanks to satisfy these heavy grazers. Supplemental algae and other vegetable matter is not difficult to provide, however. Strips of dried seaweed, formed into thin sheets, are now widely available. Those familiar with Japanese cuisine will recognize these as nori, the dried form of seaweed used to wrap sushi. Offering this marine seaweed has been found to be one of the best and most convenient ways of providing algae to saltwater fishes. Nori can also

be found in most Oriental grocery stores. There are usually two types: red and green. (The aquarium-shop choices also include brown, favored by some surgeonfishes.) I've found the green to be a better choice than the red, as it dissolves more slowly and seems to be preferred.

Nori comes in sheets or strips that can be torn to the desired size. Once this is done, the piece can simply be hung in the tank with a plastic lettuce clip, available at pet shops. For new fishes unaccustomed to eating nori, the dried seaweed can be secured to a rock with a rubber band and allowed to sink to the bottom, where the tank's inhabitants will soon start to pick at it. It may take a few attempts before your fishes get used to this food source, but once one fish begins feeding, it is usually not long before the others follow. Another attribute of nori is that it will readily soak up any fluids placed on its surface. Vitamin supplements are increasingly seen as important for marine fishes, so a few drops of liquid vitamin supplement can simply be squeezed onto the nori and allowed to soak in before feeding.

In addition to using nori, there are many other ways to offer vegetable matter to your fishes. Dried flakes of *Spirulina*, a cultured blue-green alga, are relished by many fishes and are available at all aquarium shops. Fish-food manufacturers also offer good frozen "herbivore" rations, containing marine algae, vitamins, and other green matter. Fresh vegetables from the grocery store, such as spinach and leaf lettuce (but not watery iceberg), are also used as a vegetable source by many marine aquarists. These items ought to be washed and then placed in the freezer for an hour or microwaved for approximately 30 seconds to break down the tough cellulose. Be sure to allow them to cool before feeding. (Discard any tough stemmy parts, as these will go uneaten.)

Broccoli, carrots, zucchini, and cucumbers will also be consumed by some marine species. These vegetables should be washed, peeled, and lightly blanched in boiling water before being offered. Large tangs and angelfishes appear to be particularly fond of cucumbers and zucchini, once they become accustomed to them. In no case should a serving of vegetable material be allowed to sit in the aquarium for more than 30 minutes, particularly if the fishes show no interest. Simply remove it and try a new piece at another time. It may take a dozen or more attempts to get your fishes interested in vegetables, but once they begin, many, particularly the herbivores, will often attack them greedily.

The foods added to the tank should be of appropriate sizes for the fishes being kept. If feeding chunks of shrimp, for instance, be sure to cut, chop, or grate some of the shrimp to sizes that even the smallest fishes can readily ingest. The bigger predators, such as eels or lionfishes, should also have pieces that suit their feeding habits.

On this last note, it can't be stressed too strongly that it will pay to research the feeding habits (and other biology) of the species you own. While small, active fishes may do best with several small feedings per day, large, slow predators, such as lionfishes, moray eels, and groupers, will thrive and grow on only two or three meals per week. Overfeeding will push them into rapid growth (and heavy waste production) and may shorten their lives.

VACATIONS

Never entrust the feeding of your fishes to anyone who does not understand the rules. Fish sitters are notorious for killing entire collections of marine fishes with their kindness while the owner is away. Commercial feeding blocks or time-release foods are almost useless and can easily pollute your tank. The simplest precaution is to use an automatic feeder and/or to provide your caretaker with premeasured foods you have placed in small paper or plastic cups, with one serving per cup. These can be capped or enclosed in plastic sandwich bags and placed in the freezer.

MAINTENANCE PHILOSOPHY

Once a new aquarium is up and running properly with a population of fishes, the next obvious step is to keep it this way. Without an aquarist willing to keep up with several routine tasks, even the nicest tank will lose its sparkle: algae will cover the glass, filtration gear will become fouled, water quality will decline, and serious problems, such as fish deaths, will eventually begin.

There is no way to make maintenance sound exciting, but with a proper approach and a few tricks, it can be made relatively simple and not very time-consuming. Compared to many other pet- and garden-related chores, maintaining an average marine aquarium isn't really a burden, and the rewards are immediate and satisfying. A well-maintained aquarium is always a pleasure to behold, and the grimy chores are offset by the one caretaking task that is always pleasurable: watching the tank.

WATER CHANGES

The most time-consuming and, often, the most-dreaded task is the water change. There has been much debate as to whether water changes are necessary or not, as well as how often and how much should be changed. After experimenting with just about every water-change scenario, I now employ the routine of a 5% change every other week. I've seen visible improvements in my tanks with this water-change plan, and the method described here makes the process both quicker and less tedious.

(Other equally successful aquarists have different schedules: weekly changes of 5%, biweekly changes of 10%, or even a very small daily water change—in the order of ½ to 1% of the tank's volume. Old-school hobbyists often practiced large water changes of 25 to 30%, but these tend to be more stressful on the livestock and are not recommended for typical marine aquariums except in emergencies or major rescue efforts.)

If in doubt about how much water to change, the

nitrate level and alkalinity of the system are good indicators of overall water quality. (Ammonia and nitrite should always be undetectable in an established systems as well.) If nitrate climbs above 10 to 20 ppm or alkalinity measures below 2.5 meq/L (or 7 dKH), the frequency or volume of water changes can be increased.

If you change a total of 10 to 20% per month in small weekly or every-other-week maintenance sessions, the task gets done quickly with little disruption to the system and good prospects for water-quality stability.

The first requirement for water changing is a vat or container in which to mix and age replacement water. I happen to use an old aquarium that is approximately 10% of the main tank's size. A plastic garbage can or other vessel dedicated to aquarium use is another option.

Clean tap water is mixed with aquarium salt to match the salinity of the tank and allowed to sit in the holding container for at least a couple of days with an airstone or powerhead running. The proper amount of salt needed should be weighed or measured out so that at future water changes the needed amount can simply be scooped out. (Always mixing the same volume of water and the same volume of salt to achieve the right specific gravity becomes an easy routine. Scribe your fill lines on the vat and the salt measuring container with an indelible felt marker and avoid having to measure each time.)

An airstone or a small powerhead pump, resting near the bottom of the water container, will keep the water moving and well aerated. Using a submersible heater set to the same temperature as your display aquarium is also a good idea, especially if the reserve water vat is kept in a cool basement or garage. (These are all items that you can assemble over time, and they greatly simplify the water-change chore.)

When it is time to do the change, first top up the display aquarium with freshwater, if evaporation has occurred. (Obviously, using saltwater to replenish evaporated water would quickly result in an unwanted rise in salinity.) Next, siphon the amount of water you want to replace out of the tank into a bucket and discard it. (Putting this saltwater down the drain is fine, even if you are on a septic tank. The amount of salt being discarded from a home aquarium should not be enough to cause problems.) When you have drained off the desired amount, mark the lowered water level of the tank with an indelible marker on a back (outside) corner where it is out of the way but easily seen during water changes. Then, during future changes, you can drain the tank directly into a sink, toilet, or other drain so that no hauling of buckets is necessary. For small systems or tanks not handy to a drain, this may not be necessary or possible.

Now pump or slowly pour the replacement saltwater into the system, being careful not to dislodge any of the aquascaping. To expedite the water change and to keep the time that some of the live rock may be exposed to air to a minimum, I attach a powerhead to a refill hose from the replacement-water vat. By doing this, I am able to do a 5% water change on a 400-gallon tank in less than 10 minutes.

Detritus Removal

DURING A WATER CHANGE, as much detritus, dirt, and algae as possible should be removed from the tank. Use a length of clear, flexible vinyl hose to siphon detritus from nooks and crannies in the rockwork as you remove the desired amount of water. (Some aquarists prefer a short length of rigid tubing at the end to help clean the tight spots.) An alternative method calls for a turkey baster to be used prior to the water change to help dislodge any settled detritus from the live rock. This keeps any long-term dead spots from forming and reduces the likelihood of an algal bloom. A small, hand-held powerhead can also be used to blow detritus out of the rock.

Occasionally, the substrate of the tank ought to receive a light cleaning with a gravel vacuuming tube attached to the siphon hose. Some aquarists prefer to vacuum no more than half of the substrate area at a time, to prevent a major disruption to the biological filtering capacity of the tank. With well-established live rock systems, this precaution may not be warranted. If the aquarium has a heavy fish load or if the buffering ability of the substrate has declined after long use, it may be necessary to siphon out sections of gravel from time to time and replace them with new, washed coral substrate. (Because the live rock rests directly on the bottom of the tank and not on the bed of substrate, there is no need to move or disrupt the rockwork during this procedure.)

These cleaning sessions will definitely stir up the tank and cause some temporary cloudiness, but similar events occur on the reef and are in no way harmful to the fishes or invertebrates. (If you happen to have any feather duster worms, sponges, mollusks, or other filter feeders in your tank, they will often respond positively to such particulate "storms.")

MAKEUP WATER

A WATER CHANGE IS ONLY BENEFICIAL when the new water is of higher quality than the water it is replacing. The surest tip-off of a source-water problem is the occurrence of algal blooms following water changes, as introduced nitrates, phosphates, or iron in the makeup water fuel their growth. Since water from some municipal water supplies is of less than optimum quality for marine aquariums, many serious hobbyists have found it advantageous to invest in a deionizer and/or reverse osmosis (RO) unit for water purification. These units act to remove harmful chemicals and metals from tap water. In most instances, such water purifiers are not necessary for a fish-only marine aquarium. However, if algal blooms or unexplained fish deaths are a constant battle, it may be necessary to look further into the quality of your tap water. If it is poor, finding a source of pure water may become a necessity rather than a luxury. Home-scale reverse osmosis/deionization units have become affordable and compact in recent years, but they do require some maintenance. A deionizer will need to be recharged regularly, and the membrane in the RO unit will need replacing from time to time. Note changes in a maintenance log.

TRACE ELEMENTS & SUPPLEMENTS

FOR SIMPLE FISH-ONLY MARINE systems that are not overstocked and that have the benefits of regular small water changes, the use of supplemental trace elements and other

A flexible vinyl hose can be used as a siphon to allow the tank owner to remove detritus from exposed surfaces and niches in the rockwork during routine water changes.

additives may not be required. Unlike the key elements that make up the bulk of seawater, the trace elements occur at levels of 1 ppm or less but are necessary for sustaining the health of the tank's inhabitants. For systems with reef invertebrates, especially soft or stony corals, it may be beneficial to replenish these elements on a weekly basis. There are several good trace element mixes on the market; choose one that other successful hobbyists are using. Some of these additives may cause slime algae blooms when dosed according to their directions; try starting at a dose lower than suggested and gradually titrating up.

SKIMMER CARE

WHILE MANY ASPECTS of tank maintenance require adding and subtracting things, some are simple cleaning exercises. The first thing that needs attention on a regular basis is the protein skimmer. The scum collection cup should be emptied every 3 or 4 days. While this is being done, the neck of the skimmer should also be wiped or rinsed clean. This not only makes the skimmer operate more efficiently but keeps the unit looking and smelling better (the effluent usually has an unpleasant odor, especially if allowed to collect and decay).

At a minimum, the skimmer cup and neck should be attended to weekly. If a venturi-driven model is chosen, the skimmer should also be shut off for 5 to 10 minutes every week in order to allow the venturi opening to unclog. (In a venturi skimmer, salt deposits gradually form in the air/water nozzle, causing the skimmer to lose efficiency. When the skimmer is turned off, water will flood the nozzle and dissolve the salt. This reopens the venturi and allows it to operate at peak efficiency. Periodically, the venturi should be soaked in vinegar to dissolve any accumulated calcium carbonate.) If the skimmer being used is an air-driven model, the wooden airstones will tend to get waterlogged and should be changed once a month to maintain adequately small bubbles and peak efficiency. Periodically clean the pump's air filter and replace worn diaphragms.

Lastly, the entire skimmer ought to be taken apart and cleaned every 6 months to remove the sediment that often begins to accumulate, reducing the efficiency of the unit. At the same time, clean the water pump that feeds the skimmer, rinsing the impeller in freshwater and cleaning away any accumulated slime or calcium.

ACTIVATED CARBON

ACTIVATED CARBON IS OFTEN USED to remove harmful compounds and to clear up yellowing water in a marine aquarium. Typically, one or more mesh bags of activated carbon are placed somewhere in the external filter loop where the water flow is strong. Carbon has very efficient adsorbent qualities and can quickly begin to remove all manner of dissolved and suspended matter from the water.

Because of the speed with which it can clear a tank, carbon ought to be used in a small quantity (about 2 tablespoons/10 gallons) at first. This is because the carbon will not only extract harmful compounds and clarify the water, but it may also remove needed trace elements. Sudden changes of this nature (light transmittance and water chemistry) can be stressful to any photosynthetic invertebrates as well as to macroalgae and coralline algae. Once the tank has become acclimated to having carbon present, the amount of carbon can then be increased to about 4 tablespoons/10 gallons. This should be done gradually over 2 to 3 months to prevent light shock. Once a full load of activated carbon is present, about one-half to one-third of the old carbon should be exchanged for fresh every month. (Using two or three smaller bags of carbon rather than one large one makes this task very simple.)

LIGHT BULBS

EVERY WEEK the lights and/or the lens covering the lights should be checked while they are off for any salt deposits that have accumulated. While it may appear trivial, salt buildup can dramatically reduce the amount of light being transmitted. While off, the lights should be wiped clean with a towel wetted in freshwater and then dried thoroughly. Difficult-to-remove deposits can usually be cleaned away with a solution of vinegar or isopropyl alcohol. Under no circumstances should the lights be cleaned while hot. (Cold water hitting hot lights can cause them to crack or even explode.)

In addition to cleaning the bulbs, it is also necessary

MAINTENANCE TIPS

1. Razor blades should be rinsed in freshwater after use and then placed in a sealed container with a pouch of drying silicate or some grains of rice to absorb moisture. This will reduce rust and greatly extend their usefulness.

2. Empty salt buckets (or clean plastic garbage cans) make great containers for storing newly prepared saltwater until it is needed.

3. Clean the interior of the glass and squirt debris off the rock just prior to doing a water change, allowing this suspended detritus to be siphoned out of the system.

4. Light bulbs should be turned off and allowed to cool before being cleaned. Pure water, to which a little vinegar or isopropyl alcohol has been added, works best to remove salt buildup.

---

to change them at regular intervals. Most fluorescent tubes should be changed every 6 to 9 months. Unlike incandescent bulbs, fluorescents continue to burn even when their useful life is largely over; after 9 months of typical use, aquarium fluorescent tubes can lose as much as 60% of their intensity. The exact time to change the bulbs depends not only on the bulb, but also on how long it is on every day. If your light cycle averages 12 hours, you can expect approximately 6 months of good service from your bulbs.

The importance of keeping bulbs fresh is most apparent in reef tanks with invertebrates that derive energy from light, but your viewing pleasure with a fish-only system will also diminish as bulbs age. When light-sensitive invertebrates are in the system, never replace all of your old bulbs at the same time, but rather switch one at a time, allowing a week or so to pass before the next is changed so the organisms have a chance to adapt to the new intensity gradually.

WATER TESTING

DURING THE STARTUP PHASE of a new system, frequent testing allows you to track the progress of cycling. During these initial weeks or months, you may be testing weekly for ammonia, nitrite, and nitrate.

Once the tank has cycled (with ammonia and nitrite dropping to undetectable levels), a few simple water tests should suffice each month. Some tests, such as ammonia and nitrite, need to be performed only if there appears to be a problem, such as cloudy water or the loss of livestock. If the tank continues to show readings of ammonia or nitrite, the most likely causes are overstocking or overfeeding. First, try reducing the amount of food you are providing. If this doesn't work, start increasing skimming and circulation or start lowering your fish population.

Assuming that the tank is running properly, the tests that should be done on a continuing, regular basis include temperature, salinity, nitrate, pH, and alkalinity.

The easiest measurement to take and the one most often overlooked is temperature. Taking a quick look at the thermometer several times a week (or daily, at feeding time) is a good habit to cultivate. While anything between 70 and 80 degrees F is acceptable, a good temperature range for most fish communities is 74 to 78 degrees F. If the temperature is too cool, make sure the heater is functioning properly and that it is of adequate wattage for the tank's size and the ambient room temperature. A more frequently encountered problem is that the tank is running too warm. If this is the case, once again the heater should be checked to determine if it is working properly and that the contacts are not sticking. If this is not the problem, then the excess heat is usually due to the lights not being adequately ventilated. All lights generate heat, and if the tank or the lights are not cooled by a fan, this heat will be transferred into the aquarium. If this is the problem, a small fan can be mounted to blow across the lights and the water's surface.

Pumps and powerheads can also transfer heat into the aquarium. For this reason, it may be necessary to add more fans or switch to air-cooled pumps and powerheads, particularly in the summer. In the worst case, it may be necessary to purchase a chiller or an air conditioner to cool the tank and the room. These are usually necessary only for tanks with intense lighting or in areas with extreme summer heat waves. (When the tank temperature exceeds 84 degrees F, action should be taken. Turn off the lights, and direct a fan across the surface of the water to increase evaporative cooling. For short-term emergencies, ice in tightly closed plastic bags may be floated in the tank to help moderate the temperature.)

ALKALINITY

WHILE TEMPERATURE is the easiest tank variable to measure and understand, alkalinity is one of the most difficult. Alkalinity is a measure of the buffering capacity of water, that is, how well the water resists having its pH lowered by an acid. A good alkalinity level is 2.5 to 3.5 meq/L or 7 to 10 dKH.

Over time, the buffering capacity of an aquarium will tend to decline as the buffers react with acids that are produced by ongoing decay processes. This usually occurs gradually, but it can happen quickly in a tank with a large bioload that is overfed. When this happens, normal water changes may be inadequate to maintain alkalinity, and steps need to be taken to bring the alkalinity back up to the desired level.

First, try changing more water per water change or increasing the frequency of water changes. Next, a commercial buffer may be added. There are many buffers on the market, so it is simply a matter of reading the directions and adding the chosen one accordingly. Adding or

Interior tank surfaces can be cleaned with razor or plastic blades, brushes, or other specialized aquarium cleaning devices.

Long-handled aquarist tongs are useful in larger systems for reaching deep into the tank during maintenance or feeding.

replacing some of the coral sand (aragonitc) substrate may help (see page 83). Finally, if nothing else works, the bioload should be reduced, along with the amount of food being offered.

NITRATE

ANOTHER MEASUREMENT THAT should be taken monthly is nitrate. The goal should be to have as low a level of nitrate as possible. Reef aquarists regard zero as the optimum level, although anything up to about 50 ppm is acceptable for a fish-only system. The reason to aim for very low nitrate levels (0 to 10 ppm) is that higher concentrations tend to promote the growth of algae, which is to be avoided. If your nitrates are high and algae is starting to predominate, it may be necessary to take some action, beginning with an increase in the frequency and volume of water changes. Be sure that any mechanical filter in use on the tank is being cleaned on a regular basis and that it hasn't accumulated a large amount of detritus. Next, try reducing the amount of food being added to the tank and consider cutting the bioload. (Possibly the number of specimens has climbed too high or one or more previously small specimens have become too large and are generating too much waste for the size of your system.) An alternative is to increase the size and/or the efficiency of the protein skimmer.

These measures are all attempts to reduce the amount of dissolved waste products in the tank. If these measures still do not bring your nitrate level down, then other factors may be at work. Your makeup water or salt mix may contain enough nitrate to be a source of trouble. Run a nitrate test on some of your clean replacement saltwater. If it shows a detectable level of nitrate, mix up a sample with your salt and some distilled water. If this sample tests positive for nitrate, you have established the nitrate source as the salt mix. If it is negative,

An aquarium cleaning magnet, once set in position, allows interior glass surfaces to be cleared of algal growth without having to put one's hands into the tank.

the nitrate source is your makeup water. Whatever the origin of the nitrate being introduced, steps should be taken to correct it, otherwise the growth of unwanted algae will continue to be a problem.

REMOVAL OF ALGAE

EVEN UNDER IDEAL CONDITIONS, films of algae tend to appear on the inside viewing panes of an aquarium. At least once a week, it will usually be necessary to brush or scrape this growth away. As already noted, if nitrate concentration is high, this may have to be done more frequently.

A fiber pad will usually whisk away most algae, but tougher growths may have to be zipped off with a razor blade (on glass) or a plastic scraper (on acrylic). Some aquarists like to use glass-cleaning magnet/brush sets to clean the viewing panels without getting their hands wet.

Algae that seem to be growing out of control on rocks or the substrate are best attacked with natural controls. A tang will help by grazing continuously, as will a population of snails and small hermit crabs. Brittle stars, small sea stars, and other bottom-dwelling invertebrates can also assist in keeping the sand surface algae-free.

SEMIANNUAL TASKS

A MAINTENANCE TASK THAT IS OFTEN OVERLOOKED but that should be done every 6 months is the cleaning of pumps and powerheads. Over time, detritus, slime and sometimes calcium will tend to build up on the intakes and impellers. This can seriously hamper the performance and output of the pump and shorten its life. Twice a year, the powerheads and pumps should be turned off, taken out, and thoroughly cleaned. If these units are seriously clogged, it is a good indication that they need to be cleaned more often. Once the powerheads are cleaned, their flow should noticeably increase. (After restarting newly cleaned pumps and powerheads, take note of how they are working; a suddenly increased flow can cause disruptions in the tank and unexpected skimmer activity.)

THE AQUARIUM LOG

A MARINE SYSTEM has a lot going on in a fairly small space, and keeping a record of what you observe and do is especially useful in making maintenance easier and planning for changes. This log does not need to be elaborate or complicated. All that is necessary is a method for keeping track of the tank's parameters, with dates and readings for all water tests. Also to be noted are new animals: when they are added, their approximate size, when they die, and the possible reason. Other possible entries might include your comments on the general appearance of the tank and the condition of individual specimens. All equipment changes should be recorded, particularly the dates when bulbs are changed, heaters replaced, or pumps cleaned.

Conscientious record keeping may seem rather trivial, but by having a log, it is often possible to head off problems before they get worse and, more important, de-

> "ONE LAST 'MAINTENANCE TASK' THAT SHOULD BE DONE DAILY IS TO SIT BACK AND OBSERVE THE AQUARIUM. AS SIMPLE AS THIS SOUNDS, THERE IS NO MORE IMPORTANT HABIT."
>
> ■ ■ ■

termine their cause. A written record kept in a notebook will also come in very handy when something goes wrong and you need outside advice. If you visit an aquarium shop with a tale of woe about lost fishes or excessive algal growth, the first thing they will want to know is your water test readings. Having the log will be invaluable.

In my own experience, a log proved to be a lifesaver as a diagnostic tool in determining why something bad was happening. In one instance in my show tank, which houses a large number of wrasses and anthias, a large number of these fishes (6) jumped out within a 2-week period. I was at first baffled, but my journal revealed that I had introduced a new wrasse just prior to the start of all the problems. I hadn't noticed the newcomer causing problems, because this innocent-looking wrasse never bothered any of its tankmates when the lights were on. Alerted to the possible connection between the wrasse's presence and the other fishes being harassed, I staged a night vigil. Sure enough, once the lights went down, this fish became the neighborhood bully. After the wrasse was removed, the unscheduled flights ceased. Granted, I probably would have realized what was happening sooner or later, but my log gave me an early clue that this fish might be the culprit.

Besides being a convenient record of tank conditions and what has been done, the log can also serve as a reminder of future tasks. Make a note of how often maintenance jobs need to be performed, and then schedule them accordingly, e.g., water changes biweekly, bulb changes every 9 months, and so on. When tasks are regularly scheduled and called for on a set date, they are more likely to be carried out. It is the unscheduled "emergency" maintenance that seems to come up at the most inopportune moments and that takes up the most time.

THE ULTIMATE "CHORE"

ONE LAST "MAINTENANCE TASK" that should be done daily is to sit back and observe the aquarium. As simple as this sounds, there is no more important habit. The

UPGRADING AN EXISTING UNDERGRAVEL-FILTER SYSTEM

The health and appearance of an established aquarium can be greatly improved by adding live rock and reducing the tank's dependence on undergravel filtration. This may be done in one major overhaul or over a period of months. (Never add uncured live rock to an established aquarium with fishes or invertebrates present.)

COMPLETE OVERHAUL

1. Start quarantine tank.

2. Acquire cured live rock (or cure your own in a separate container) and any additional required equipment (see pages 80 to 81).

3. Shut down display tank and move all fishes and decorative corals to the quarantine system.

4. Remove all sand and undergravel plates. Completely clean tank or allow to settle and siphon out as much detritus as possible. Rinse sand in warm, clean, aged saltwater and save for reuse.

5. Add live rock, followed by rinsed, bacteria-filled sand from the original system. (Follow the step-by-step procedure for starting and cycling a new tank, pages 73 to 85.)

6. Restart equipment and allow system to cycle while fishes remain in quarantine tank.

7. Reintroduce fishes from quarantine tank in stages, properly acclimating them to the new conditions.

ON THE FLY

If doing a total overhaul is not an appealing scenario, an existing undergravel system can be converted to live rock biological filtration without removing the tank's population of fishes.

1. Siphon off the substrate until only ½ to 1 inch remains above the undergravel plate. This can be done all at once or gradually during water changes.

(If possible, remove detritus that has accumulated under the plate as well.)

2. Remove all existing decorations and replace with fully cured live rock. The rock can be placed on the old substrate, with the undergravel plate remaining in place and continuing to run.

3. Install protein skimmer, new lighting, powerheads, and other equipment. (The new equipment can be added either before or after the live rock is added, or may be brought on in stages.)

4. After introducing the live rock, test for ammonia and nitrite and allow undergravel filter to continue running until tank conditions are completely settled.

5. Once ammonia and nitrite show no detectable presence, disconnect power (air or powerheads) to the undergravel filter. If possible, remove lift tubes and cap off entrances to the undergravel plenum. Leave undergravel plates in place.

These additions and changes will go a long way toward improving the water quality of the tank. This system should be stable for an extended period, but it may be necessary to lift the rock and siphon off the detritus underneath it from time to time or to remove the undergravel plates altogether.

The best alternative is still to remove the plate from the tank at some point. The substrate is quite viable and full of bacteria and should be retained.

---

mental checklist usually covers water clarity, equipment performance, a head count of fishes, and an assurance that all are eating and behaving normally. Only by regularly watching the aquarium will the owner get an appreciation for how the tank and its occupants are doing. Frequent observations allow one to get a sense of when things are going right or if something is amiss. These viewing sessions will often pinpoint a potential problem

long before it can blossom into a catastrophe.

The upkeep of a marine aquarium, if the owner settles into a regular routine (at least a few daily minutes of observation, with a short work session at a fixed time each week), should be almost automatic. For many of us, it becomes a relaxing, almost therapeutic time, with results that we—and everyone else who watches our aquarium—will see and appreciate.

CHAPTER 7

HEALTH

Preventing and Curing Common Disease and Parasite Problems

EVEN IN THE BEST OF AQUARIUMS, AS IN the healthiest homes, diseases can happen. However, in a thriving aquarium where fish are well acclimated, well nourished and free of stress, disease can be a very uncommon occurrence. When care is exercised to prevent sudden changes or contamination by new specimens, the loss of fishes in an established system to parasites or diseases should be extremely rare.

In my own experience, the riskiest time for losing a specimen is within 30 days of purchase. It is during this first month that a new fish must recover from the accumulated stresses of being collected, shipped thousands of miles, being passed through many sets of hands (collector, buyer, exporter, importer, distributor, local re-

Left: a good local aquarium shop is often the best resource to consult for disease problems. **Above:** juvenile Queen Angelfish.

tailer, and the aquarist)—often with less than ideal water conditions through much of the journey.

Eventually some of these fishes will become sick. The good news is that there are only a relatively few diseases that the average marine aquarist is ever likely to see. These have treatments, and if the problem is caught early and the fish is isolated, there is often a very good chance for complete recovery. To ensure that a new fish does not bring new problems into your display aquarium—where it can infect all the other specimens and where it cannot be treated—it should go through a few weeks of home quarantine.

A simple quarantine setup (see page 114) is the aquarist's best defense against bringing pathogens into a thriving aquarium. Of the diseases most likely to afflict new fishes, the three most common are marine velvet (*Amyloodinium ocellatum*), marine ich (*Cryptocaryon irritans*), and clownfish disease (*Brooklynella hostilis*).

Marine velvet is caused by a dinoflagellate alga, while marine ich and *Brooklynella* are caused by ciliated protozoans. All of these parasitic diseases can be fatal if left untreated, but marine velvet infestations are usually more virulent and may even wipe out an entire tank.

MARINE VELVET

MARINE VELVET (*Amyloodinium ocellatum*), also known as coral fish disease, *Oodinium*, and incorrectly as saltwater ich, appears as a powdery film or, with closer inspection, as very tiny white dots (0.02 to 0.08 mm in diameter) on the fish's skin. The initial outbreak will usually go unnoticed because if there are only a few of the parasites present, they will be hard to see. After a few days, however, these parasites will drop off the fish as cysts (called tomonts) and go into a reproductive stage. During this 3-day period, each cyst will divide so that when it ruptures it will release over 250 new subadult organisms (called tomites). These free-swimming parasites will then spend the next 2 days looking for a fish host; if one is not found, they will die. Unfortunately, in a closed environment like an aquarium, a host is readily available. Quickly covered with attached tomites, the fish will appear to be covered with whitish velvet. Each tomite transforms into a trophont, which feeds by liquefying small areas of the fish's skin or gills. After a few days, the trophonts drop off, enter the reproductive stage, and soon release thousands more tomites. An infected fish will often scratch itself against rocks or gravel and may appear to be gasping for breath. Respiratory difficulties increase, eventually leading to listlessness, respiratory arrest, and death.

The cure requires removing the infected fish to a quarantine aquarium for treatment if it isn't already in isolation. The treatment of choice for this disease (and also for *Cryptocaryon irritans*) is copper sulfate. This compound is not only toxic to the *Amyloodinium* alga, but it is toxic to virtually all of the organisms present on the live rock. Copper sulfate, especially the citrated form

> "THE GOOD NEWS IS THAT THERE ARE ONLY A RELATIVELY FEW DISEASES THAT THE AVERAGE MARINE AQUARIST IS EVER LIKELY TO SEE."
>
> ■ ■ ■

(SeaCure is the old standby), is a very effective drug, but it should not be used in the display aquarium or it will kill any invertebrates, macroalgae, and desirable organisms on the live rock. Copper can be used continuously in the quarantine tank, however, as its impact on the biological filter is tolerable. The goal is to maintain a treatment level of about 0.15 ppm of ionic copper during a treatment period of 14 to 21 days.

Amyloodinium is so debilitating that some fish infected will be too sick to put up much resistance to being caught. Unfortunately, if the fish cannot be removed, it is probably destined to perish and is very likely to infect the other fishes in the tank (see Catching Fishes, page 136).

Once a diseased fish has been captured, it should be acclimated to the water in the quarantine tank and then treated with copper sulfate for 2 to 3 weeks. (Some aquarists recommend a 3-minute dip in freshwater before treatment with copper.) The level of copper should be checked daily with a copper test kit, and the copper level adjusted accordingly to maintain the desired level. Unfortunately some fishes, such as mandarins, butterflyfishes, clownfishes, and pygmy angelfishes (notably the Flame Angelfish), do not tolerate copper very well; it may be necessary to treat these fishes at lower copper doses over a longer period of time.

After the infected fish has been isolated, some steps need to be taken to reduce the presence of the disease in the display tank. These steps may also need to be taken should any of the other infectious diseases occur. First, the specific gravity will need to be dropped to between 1.012 and 1.010 for at least 3 weeks. This can be done is steps. Remove about 5% of the system water and replace it with aged freshwater that has been brought to the same temperature as the aquarium. Wait about 3 hours, test with a hydrometer, and repeat until the desired level is reached. (To be very safe, this dilution of the system water can be done over a longer period to avoid overstressing any invertebrate inhabitants in the tank.) The drop in salinity will usually be well tolerated by all of the fishes.

(Sharks and rays are an exception, and valuable delicate invertebrates, such as corals, should be removed to another system during the treatment to be completely safe.)

This lowering of salinity will reduce the amount of work that the fishes need to do to remove excess salt from their bodies and will give them more stamina to fight off parasites.

To eradicate parasites buried in the sand, the substrate can be removed and soaked in freshwater for 2 weeks. This will kill off any cysts that are resting in the substrate as well as limiting the sites for any left in the tank. An ultraviolet sterilizer or ozone may be used to treat the display tank water to reduce the population of free-swimming pathogens. All of this will greatly reduce the likelihood of the entire tank becoming infected. These steps may only need to be undertaken should several fish show signs of being infected.

An alternate method of making an infected tank safe is to remove all the fishes and let the system run for at least a month while the parasite population crashes, due to a lack of hosts.

Obviously, it is much better to keep this lethal disease from getting into your aquarium in the first place. Many aquarists who have learned the hard way can attest that quarantine tanks and isolation procedures can spare a great deal of work, expense, and loss of fish life.

MARINE ICH

A DISEASE THAT IS SOMETIMES CONFUSED with marine velvet, but which is fortunately less infectious and less virulent, is marine ich (*Cryptocaryon irritans*), also known as saltwater ich. As with marine velvet, the fish looks irritated and is constantly trying to scratch itself. The *Cryptocaryon* parasite, however, is easier to see, as it is the size of a pinhead (0.3 to 0.5 mm) and appears as discrete white specks like grains of salt on the fish's body (not as an opaque film, characteristic of *Amyloodinium*). The treatment for *Cryptocaryon*, however, is the same as that for *Amyloodinium*: move the infected fish to the quarantine tank and treat it with citrated copper sulfate. However, since these fishes aren't normally as ill and debilitated as those infected with marine velvet, they will be more difficult to catch. Fortunately, lowering the salinity as described above and doing more fre-

---

TOXIC DRUGS

Copper, formalin, methylene blue, malachite green, and many other common aquarium remedies are deadly to invertebrates and will kill snails, brittle stars, feather duster worms, and the like—not to mention clams and corals in reef aquariums. They will also destroy at least part of the microbial population that drives the biological filter. The ammonia caused by the death of invertebrates and the loss of beneficial bacteria can create a toxic water situation with suddenly elevated ammonia and possibly nitrite levels. This can seriously worsen the disease situation already in progress.

Treating fishes in the display aquarium with copper or most other antiparasitic, antibacterial, or antifungal drugs is almost never a good idea. The aquarist must get the afflicted specimens out of the tank and into a quarantine treatment system where they can be safely medicated.

---

quent water changes and feeding medicated foods along with vitamin supplements may be enough to limit problems from this pathogen if it appears in a display tank.

In severe cases of *Cryptocaryon* infection, the fish should be removed from the system and given a 10-to-15-minute dip in a solution of formalin (2 teaspoons of 37% formaldehyde per gallon of heavily aerated saltwater) before being placed in a treatment or quarantine tank with copper sulfate.

CLOWNFISH DISEASE

BROOKLYNELLA HOSTILIS is a pathogen that, up until recently, was primarily seen in clownfishes—particularly the Maroon Clown (*Premnas biaculeatus*). This accounts for its common name, clownfish disease. Curiously, it is now reported to be affecting angelfishes and damselfishes as well. *Brooklynella* usually attacks fishes immediately after importation, manifesting as a whitish gray film or coat of mucus covering the fish. Other symptoms include loss of appetite, rapid breathing, and gasping.

The infected fish usually displays symptoms while it is undergoing its initial quarantine period. It should be removed from the quarantine tank and given a dip in freshwater, or saltwater with formalin, or saltwater with a mixture of formalin and malachite green. Unless you are familiar with pharmaceuticals and know how to calculate dosages, buy brands of these drugs that are prepared for aquarium usage and follow the directions that accompany them. Leave the infected fish in the dip bucket for 5 minutes or until it shows signs of distress (e.g., heavy breathing, lying on its side, frantically trying to jump out). After the dip, the fish should be returned to the quarantine tank. Dipping should be repeated 1 to 2 times daily for 7 to 10 days until no signs of the disease

are present. (Rather than dipping, some aquarists prefer to treat *Brooklynella*-afflicted fishes in the quarantine tank itself. The medications being used will reduce the populations of beneficial bacteria in the sponge filter, so it will be necessary to do regular water changes to keep ammonia levels under control.)

CLOUDY EYE & POPEYE

OCCASIONALLY A FISH WILL DEVELOP a cloudy or opaque eye or eyes. In many of these cases the problem is bacterial in nature. Bacterial infections in aquariums can be very difficult to treat, but the best hope is to get some oral antibiotics into the affected fish(es).

The easiest way to do this is to mix an antibiotic such as tetracycline into some highly palatable blended frozen food. Allow 1 to 2 ounces of frozen food to thaw until it reaches a liquid consistency. At this point, half of a 100 to 250 mg capsule of tetracycline should be mixed into the food and allowed to dissolve. The food should then be re-frozen. This medicated food should be given to the infected fish(es) in small portions for approximately 14 days, after which time the cloudiness should be gone.

Another eye malady, called popeye, is indicated by one or both eyes bulging noticeably, as if under pressure. This may be the result of a physical injury, or it may be bacterial or fungal in nature. Time often heals the bruised eye, but in some cases, the fish may lose the eye and die. A course of oral tetracycline, chloramphenicol, or kanamycin may be warranted if the problem is severe or if both eyes are involved.

Poor water quality has been suggested as a possible precursor to eye infections that appear in display tanks, and a program of 5 to 10% daily water changes may be in order until conditions improve.

LYMPHOCYSTIS

APPEARING AS SMALL, IRREGULAR WHITE CLUMPS on a fish's fins, lips, or body, lymphocystis is sometimes described as looking like bits of cauliflower. It is a viral disease, and there are no known drug treatments. Fortunately, lymphocystis usually disappears over time and seems to cause few mortalities, although it can sometimes increase the fish's susceptibility to other, more lethal diseases. Cleaner wrasses will sometimes nibble away the growths, and some expert aquarists remove them surgically, although the procedure can be very stressful for the fish and may even cause the virus to spread. Like a temporary case of warts, lymphocystis usually disappears within a number of weeks and the fish will be no worse for the infection.

GASTROINTESTINAL INFECTIONS & WORMS

A GASTROINTESTINAL INFECTION may only become evident once a fish is in quarantine. Signs of this are feces that are white and either stringy or slimy. Treatment with a wide-spectrum antibiotic such as tetracycline may help (see treatment regimen under Cloudy Eye & Popeye, page 136).

Internal parasites can also produce similar symptoms, as well as wasting or emaciation, suggesting a gastrointestinal worm infestation or trematodes. Some success in treating these problems has been reported with fishes kept at a low salinity for several weeks and given food containing piperazine or praziquantel, both of which kill a wide variety of worms. During this treatment, frozen plankton is thawed in water containing half a capsule of one of these drugs. After sitting in the water for several minutes, the plankton takes up some of the medication. The plankton is then given to the infested fishes for 1 to 2 weeks until symptoms are no longer present.

Clearly, it is difficult and time consuming to manage and cure a diseased fish. This is why the importance of a quarantine tank should not be downplayed. To do a cost/benefit analysis is relatively simple. If the average marine aquarium houses 10 fishes with an average price of $30/fish, the total livestock investment is $300. A small quarantine tank may cost no more than $50 to set up and maintain for an entire year. So for less than the cost of two fishes, the display tank can be kept virtually free of disease as long as all new fishes are properly quarantined. The result: little risk of the entire tank being wiped out—not to mention the time and energy invested by the aquarist in putting that collection of fishes together. From a simple economic standpoint, it is readily apparent that a properly used quarantine tank will more than pay for itself.

HEAD & LATERAL LINE EROSION

ONE MALADY THAT MAY OCCUR long after a fish has settled happily into the display tank—and months after quarantine—is head and lateral line erosion (HLLE), also called lateral line disease or hole-in-the-head disease. As the names imply, this problem manifests itself along the lateral line and/or on the head of the fish, as marked necrosis (tissue erosion), which progresses over time. Causes for this disease have been postulated as everything from excessive carbon use, poor diet, and lack of vitamin C to stray electrical voltage. The fishes most frequently afflicted are tangs and angelfishes.

Some recent reports indicate that HLLE has been successfully treated by increasing the amount of vegetable matter in the affected fish's diet. Some suggest feeding dried seaweed that has been soaked with a liquid vitamin supplement containing vitamins A, C, and D. (Iodine may also help.) This treatment is said to reverse the disease and grow back much of the tissue on the fish's face and sides. Unfortunately, if significant tissue loss has occurred, some scarring may remain.

OTHER HEALTH PROBLEMS

AS WITH HUMANS, fishes have a tremendous number of potential health problems. Thankfully, even long-term aquarists only rarely see most fish diseases. These uncommon maladies include dropsy, fungal infections, *Glugea* in certain species, large external parasites, viral diseases, and others. If unusual symptoms appear in your system, consult a book on aquarium fish diseases or talk to a knowledgeable staff member at your local aquarium shop. (Most veterinarians have little or no experience with marine fishes, so seeking professional intervention is usually impossible or impractical. If a veterinarian who treats fishes is available in your area, your aquarium store will probably know about it.)

Of course the best medicine for virtually all fish diseases is prevention: buying healthy stock, keeping your water quality high, avoiding sudden shifts of temperature, pH, or specific gravity, and running all new fishes through a quarantine tank where most incoming problems can be stopped before they spread. These simple measures, followed faithfully, will help assure an environment appreciated by both you and your captive charges.

CONTACTS

WEB SITES

American Marinelife Dealers Association
    www.amdareef.com
Aqualink Aquaria Web Resources
    www.aqualink.com
Breeder's Registry for Marine Aquarium
Cultured Fishes and Invertebrates
    www.breeders-registry.gen.ca.us
Compuserve Aquaria/Fish Forum
    petsforum.com
Coral Reef Aquaculture Sites
    farmedcoral.homestead.com
International Marinelife Alliance
    www.imamarinelife.org
Marine Aquarium Council (MAC)
    www.aquariumcouncil.org
#Reefs (Reef Aquarium Forum)
    www.reefs.org
Reef Central
    www.reefcentral.com
U.S. Government Coral Reef Task Force
    coralreef.gov

PERIODICALS

Aquarium Fish Magazine
Russ Case, Editor
Fancy Publications
P.O. Box 6050
Mission Viejo, CA 92690-6050
(949) 855-8822
Web site: www. animalnetwork.com/fish

Aquarium Frontiers On-Line
Terry Siegel, Editor
Web site: www.animalnetwork.com

Freshwater and Marine Aquarium
Patricia Crews, Editor
144 West Sierra Madre Boulevard
Sierra Madre, CA 91024
(818) 355-1476
Web site: www.mag-web.com/fama

Journal of MaquaCulture
Stanley Brown, Editor
P.O. Box 255373
Sacramento, CA 95865-5373

Marine Fish Monthly
Boyce Phipps, Editor
3243 Highway 61 East
Luttrell, TN 37779
e-mail: pubcon@worldnet.att.net

Practical Fishkeeping
Steve Windsor, Editor
EMAP Pursuit Publishing
Bretton Court
Bretton, Peterborough
PE3 8DZ United Kingdom
011-44-1733-264666

SeaScope
Thomas A. Frakes, Editor
Aquarium Systems, Inc.
8141 Tyler Boulevard
Mentor, OH 44060
Web site: www.aquariumsystems.com

Tropical Fish Hobbyist
Mary Sweeney, Editor
One T.F.H. Plaza
Neptune City, NJ 07753
(732) 988-8400
e-mail: info@tfh.com
Web site: www.tfh.com

MASNA

Marine Aquarium Societies of North America
c/o Nancy Swart
31 Lagoon Drive
Hawthorn Woods, IL 60047
Web site: www.masna.org
Umbrella association of city, regional and state marine aquarium groups in the United States and Canada, with individual memberships for aquarists who do not belong to a local society.

AUTHOR & EDITOR

Michael S. Paletta, Author
James M. Lawrence, Editor
Microcosm Ltd.
P.O. Box 550
Charlotte, VT 05445
(802) 425-5700
e-mail: jml@microcosm-books.com
Web site: www.microcosm-books.com

BIBLIOGRAPHY

Adey, W.H. and K. Loveland. 1991. *Dynamic Aquaria: Building Living Ecosystems.* Academic Press, Inc., San Diego, CA.

Allen, G. 1985. *Butterfly and Angelfishes of the World Vol. 2.* Aquarium Systems, Mentor, OH.

Allen, G. 1991. *Damselfishes of the World.* Aquarium Systems, Mentor, OH.

Amlacher, E. 1970. *Textbook of Fish Diseases.* Tropical Fish Hobbyist Publications, Neptune City, NJ.

Axelrod, H.R., W.E. Burgess, and R. Hunziker. 1990. *Atlas of Aquarium Fishes Reference Book.* Tropical Fish Hobbyist Publications, Neptune City, NJ.

Blasiola, G.C. 1992. Diseases of ornamental marine fishes. In Gratzek, J.B. and J.R. Matthews, Eds. *Aquariology: The Science of Fish Health Management.* Tetra Press, Morris Plains, NJ.

Burleson, J. 1987. Miniature reef aquarium lighting. *SeaScope* Vol. 4, Fall.

Dakin, N. 1992. *The Book of the Marine Aquarium.* Tetra Press, Blacksburg, VA.

Debelius, H. and H. Baensch. 1994. *Marine Atlas Vol. 1.* Mergus, Melle, Germany, and Microcosm Ltd., Shelburne, VT.

Debelius, H. 1986. *Fishes for the Invertebrate Aquarium.* Meinders and Elstermann, Osnabrück, Germany.

Delbeek, J.C. 1992. Dutch minireefs: an update. *Aquarium Fish Magazine* 4(11) 52-59.

Delbeek, J.C. 1998. Marine aquarium filtration. *Aquarium USA.* 34-45.

Delbeek, J.C. and J.F. Sprung. 1994. *The Reef Aquarium.* Ricordea Publishing, Coconut Grove, FL.

Dustan, P. Depth-dependent photoadaption by zooxanthellae of the reef coral *Montastrea annularis. Mar. Biol.* 68:253-264.

Emmens, C.W. 1975. *The Marine Aquarium in Theory and Practice.* Tropical Fish Hobbyist Publications, Neptune City, NJ.

Emmens, C.W. 1986. The natural system and the minireef. *Freshwater and Marine Aquarium* 9:71.

Eng, L.C. 1961. Nature's system of keeping marine fishes. *Tropical Fish Hobbyist* 9(6) 23-30.

Fossa, S. and A. Nilsen. 1996. *The Modern Coral Reef Aquarium.* Birgit Schmettkamp Verlag, Bornheim, Germany.

Frakes, T. 1993. Red Sea Reef "Mesocosms" in Monaco. *SeaScope* Vol. 11(3), Summer.

Harker, R. 1997. Lighting for the artificial reef. *Aquarium Frontiers* May/June, 1997.

Haywood, M. and S. Wells. 1989. *The Manual of Marine Invertebrates.* Tetra Press, Morris Plains, NJ.

Headlee, L., L. Read, and N. Barnes. 1996. Superglue use in live rock culture. *SeaScope* Vol. 13, Spring.

Hovanec, T.A. 1993. All about activated carbon. *Aquarium Fish Magazine* 5(8): 54-63.

Kirk, J.T. 1994. *Light and Photosynthesis in Aquatic Ecosystems.* Cambridge University Press, Cambridge, UK.

Kollman, R. 1998. Low salinity as quarantine and treatment of marine fish parasites. *SeaScope* Vol. 15, Spring.

Mills, D. 1985. *A Fishkeeper's Guide to Marine Fish.* Salamander Press, London.

Moe, M. 1989. *Marine Aquarium Reference: Systems and Invertebrates.* Green Turtle Publications, Plantation, FL.

Moe, M. 1992. *Marine Aquarium Handbook.* Green Turtle Publications, Plantation, FL.

Nilsen, A. 1990. The successful coral reef aquarium, Parts 1, 2, 3, 4. *Freshwater and Marine Aquarium* 13(9, 10, 11, 12).

Nilsen, A. 1991. Coral reef vs. reef aquarium. *Aquarium Fish Magazine* 4(1) 18-26.

Paletta, M. 1990. Eliminating problem algae. *SeaScope* Vol. 7, Fall.

Paletta, M.S. and R. Hildreth. 1997. The ecosystem filtration method. *SeaScope* Vol. 14, Summer.

Riddle, D. 1995. *The Captive Reef.* Energy Savers Unlimited, Harbor City, CA.

Riddle, D. 1996. Water movement: From the coral reef to the reef tank. *Aquarium Frontiers* 3(4).

Smit, G. 1986. Marine aquariums, part one: Is it time for a change? *Freshwater and Marine Aquarium* 9(1) 35-42.

Spotte, S. 1973. *Marine Aquarium Keeping: The Science, Animals and Art.* John Wiley and Sons, Inc., New York.

Steene, R. 1985. *Butterfly and Angelfishes of the World Vol 1.* Aquarium Systems, Mentor, OH.

Tullock, J. 1997. *Natural Reef Aquariums.* Microcosm Ltd., Shelburne, VT.

Van Ommen, J. 1992. Light above saltwater aquariums. *Het Zee Aquarium* 42(3) 59-63.

Wilkens, P. 1973. *The Saltwater Aquarium for Tropical Marine Invertebrates.* Engelbert Pfriem Verlag, Wuppertal, Germany.

PHOTOGRAPHY &
ILLUSTRATION CREDITS

EDWARD KADUNC
All illustrations

SCOTT W. MICHAEL
Front cover, 44, 45, 73, 86, 90, 91, 92, 93,
94, 95, 96, 97, 98, 100, 101, 102, 103, 104,
105, 106, 107, 108 (TL, TR), 117, 133
Back cover (species photographs)

JOHN GOODMAN
10, 11, 19, 29, 60, 72, 84, 87, 118, 119,
125, 128, 129, 132, 144

CHARLES CARPENTIER
61, 62, 65, 66, 67, 71

STEVE LUCAS FOR EXOTIC AQUARIA/ORA
27, 28, 56, Back cover (C)

MAX GIBBS/PHOTOMAX
12, 13

JANINE CAIRNS-MICHAEL
108 (B)

MICHAEL S. PALETTA
17

WAYNE SHANG/FREMONT, CA
15

JEFFREY TURNER FOR EXOTIC AQUARIA/ORA
18

INDEX

ABOUT THE AUTHOR

MICHAEL S. PALETTA is one of North America's leading amateur marine aquarists and a frequent contributor to *Aquarium Fish Magazine*, *SeaScope*, and *Aquarium Frontiers*. He has been involved in the design and setup of more than 60 marine aquariums, including the 4,500-gallon reef exhibit at the National Aquarium in Baltimore and a number of reef systems at the Pittsburgh Zoo Aquarium. He has a degree in biology, psychology, and chemistry from Dickinson College and holds a master's degree in psycho-pharamacology from Yale University. He works in the field of biotechnology and lives with his family near Pittsburgh, Pennsylvania.